THE BUG IN OUR THINKING

Also by Hugh Willbourn

Agree to Win, BBC Books

I Can Mend Your Broken Heart, Bantam Press (with Paul McKenna)

THE BUG IN OUR THINKING

AND THE WAY TO FIX IT

HUGH WILLBOURN

First published 2023.

ISBN 978-1-7393511-0-6

WELWYN PRESS

I thank all my family, friends and colleagues who have been supportive, if sometimes perplexed, over many years.

I owe special thanks to two people who have listened to me and encouraged me through countless, lengthy iterations of this project: to my thoughtful, generous friend and business partner David Corr, and to my wife, Lê Minh Hiếu.

CONTENTS

PROLOGUE

This is the story of an involuntary discovery that unfolded over thirty years. It is about something so small with consequences so vast that it changed the way we think.

There is a very good reason why it is hard to focus on and hard to write about. It is a little bit easier to discuss face to face, but it still isn't easy. Perhaps one day we will meet and we can talk about it. I hope that happens.

As you read there will be countless opportunities to dispute and disagree, or think me foolish or ignorant or unbalanced or unscientific or absurd.

Before you turn away, ask yourself,

'What could he be *trying* to say?'

'Maybe this is not the whole story, but could there be something to it?'

'If these points were made properly, the way a sensible person would make them, could I find something valuable here?'

1

CASTLES AND WINDSURFERS

Just as I reached the bottom of the tenement stairs a door banged open and a woman ran out into the courtyard screaming, 'Help! Help! He's gonna kill me!'

She ran across to a passageway of steps up to the street.

In pursuit ran her furious boyfriend shouting, 'You f**king bitch!'

She ran up the steps and barged past an old couple who were on the landing halfway down. The boyfriend was just a few yards behind. As he passed the couple the old man pushed out his walking stick. The boyfriend tripped and fell hard, flat on his face. He stayed down for a couple of seconds. He stood up dazed and still angry but the blind rage had gone.

The old couple walked on.

The woman got away.

The story could end there.

But it could continue.

Soon after that incident boyfriend and girlfriend split up. The woman took up with another man who soon became her pimp. The boyfriend raised their little boy on his own. When I bumped into them in the neighbourhood he always seemed happy. I never saw him angry again.

Early in my psychotherapeutic career I had a client who was very polite, had never had a romance and did not like her job. She had a well-crafted mask of social acceptability.

She was depressed.

In our first session I suggested that before our next meeting she do some little thing, anything, which she found embarrassing. Of course she didn't. Several years later she told me that she was so frightened she almost didn't come back.

At her next session she told me how her mother had taught her not to trust people, to be fearful and to keep herself safe.

Some people create their safety by building a castle. They make a wall of protective habits and avoidance. The walls are strong and thick so that they are safe from any attack. It works very well.

The downside is twofold. First, it is constant work to maintain the defences and keep people at a distance. Secondly, it gets lonely. The defences that keep dangers and strangers away also prevent friends and lovers getting close.

I put it to my client that she had built herself a very strong castle.

She agreed.

I told her about my attempts to windsurf. I am a perpetual beginner, so I have taken many lessons. The first step is to get up on your board. You are standing about waist-deep in the water with the board in front of you. You climb on to it and immediately fall off. It takes several attempts before you can keep your balance. The next stage is to kneel and then stand up. You try. You fall back into the water.

Eventually, you achieve it. You are standing on your board! Now you have to pull up the mast and sail. You pull on the rope, the sail and the mast rise up and splash! Once again, there is more falling off before you are able to raise the mast. All this falling off, climbing back on board, standing up and pulling the sail is tiring, and still you are not going anywhere. To sail you have to get hold of the boom and pull it round to catch the wind. So you try to do that and go back in the water. When eventually you succeed the feeling is wonderful. You are sailing!

Soon, however, you realize you must change direction, otherwise you will run aground or disappear over the horizon. You need to swing the sail around. The first, and probably the second, third and fourth times you try to do that, you fall off.

At every single stage of learning to windsurf you fall off. You have to climb back up and keep trying until you can keep your balance through each manoeuvre.

You will still fall from time to time, but you become quicker at getting going again.

Now when you are sailing the very things that caused you to fall off become your allies. The wind is your power and the waves are your playthings.

A windsurfer is exposed to everything that the sea and the weather has to offer. It is your responsiveness to the forces around you that keep you safe.

Where the castle builder achieves security by shutting out the world, the windsurfer gains security by becoming more and more connected to the environment.

My client listened to me with her ever-so-slightly-puzzled expression. I don't know if that helped her, but something did. In due course she left her job, moved house and made new friends.

Everything you need to know has already been written. You just need to find it.

And understand it.

I learned a great deal from my early hypnotherapy clients. My very first client had a phobia of vomiting. I hypnotized her and removed the phobia. I asked her to come back in a week just to check all was well. She came back and told me it had worked brilliantly. The phobia had totally disappeared. But then she got it back the day before our second meeting.

'How did that happen?' I asked her.

'Oh,' she said. 'It's how I control my husband.'

More experienced psychotherapists refer to benefits derived from apparent complaints as 'secondary gain'.

My naivety was not always problematic. A young man came to see me. I can no longer remember what his presenting problem was, maybe I didn't even understand it at the time, but he definitely wanted hypnosis so I put him into a trance. I was not sure what to do next, so I told him that he was a great guy. He was talented, sensitive and intelligent. He was valuable and lovable. I looked forward to hearing of his success. I told him in several different ways that he had strength and resilience and willingness to learn, to work and to love.

Then I woke him up.

He paused for a moment or two, then he said,

'I've been waiting my whole life for somebody to tell me that.'

What if there is a reason why so many things go wrong? What if that reason is so ancient, so simple and so unbelievable that if I told it to you right now you would laugh?

The greatest hypnotist of the 20th century was an American psychiatrist named Milton H. Erickson. As a child Erickson was paralysed by polio. He remobilized himself by using mental effort and vivid muscle memory to reinforce minute movements that he observed in his own body. At medical school he conducted extensive studies of both hypnotic trance and suggestibility and developed a novel approach to therapy. In his practice he used both hypnosis and the wider social context of his clients to achieve extraordinary cures of both physical and psychological ailments. He advised his students,

'Always use what the client brings.'

Erickson's collected works run to four volumes: two volumes of research and two volumes of clinical practice and case histories. I've read every single page and in all those four volumes he never once advances a theory of hypnosis.

In his later years Erickson was renowned as a teacher and therapists would come from all over America to sit and listen to him. In reply to almost every question about hypnosis, Erickson would tell a story.

Uncommon Therapy is an excellent introduction to Erickson's work written by Jay Haley. Haley himself became pretty famous and much in demand at conferences. At one event a therapist approached him for help and explained she was having trouble working with a mother and daughter who were symbiotically attached to one another. Haley replied,

'I'd never let that be the problem.'

What did he mean by that? We will get back to it. I promise.

In the first quarter of the 21st century we have more people more educated than ever in human history. We have more graduates, more PhDs, more scientists, analysts and economists than ever before; we have more wealth, more technology and more access to unprecedented amounts of knowledge, yet we are making a mess all over the world. What is the problem? And why hasn't all that education improved things?

On the morning of Christmas day 2009 I received a phone call from a complete stranger. He introduced himself as a health and safety consultant and said, 'I've just read the report you wrote for the Health and Safety Executive and I had to ring to tell you that it is the best bloody HSE report I've ever read!'

At that time I had a qualitative market research partnership with David Corr. The report in question was an investigation into operators of small building sites. (You can find it if you google 'Corr Willbourn HSE small construction site operators.') I was flattered that our work had prompted his call and thanked him. Later I realized that the credit really belonged to the builders we had interviewed.

All the builders we talked to knew about health and safety and all were glad that many dangerous practices of the bad old days had been banned. They all tried to work safely. They had all witnessed accidents caused by stupidity and carelessness and some even caused by complacency inadvertently created by health and safety practice.

The HSE collects data and compiles statistics on accidents. They analyse the data to identify contributory factors and create regulations to eliminate those factors.

The builders' attitudes were founded in their own experience. Most of them had served an apprenticeship and all of them had many years, in some cases many decades, in the trade.

The builders understood that the Health and Safety Executive was telling them, 'Follow all of these regulations. Do A and B and C ... and X and Y and Z, and your building site will be a safe place to work.'

Deep down they didn't believe the Health and Safety Executive. They thought a better message was, 'Remember, it's dangerous!'

Do you get the feeling you are not sure where this is going?

Why isn't there a proper introduction? Good question. Here are some more:

Is there a good reason why things are a bit vague at this point?

What if something misleading was built into your thinking without your knowledge and we had to tread very carefully to escape it?

It is as though when you opened this book a great number of jigsaw pieces fell out in a pile on the floor. There is no picture to guide you. Maybe these pieces here fit together, but it may not be clear what they show. There will be more pieces that don't seem to fit but in a little while some parts of the picture will appear.

Life is like that.

Sometime in the early 1990s I happened to hear Derek Jameson interview Allen Carr. Jameson was an East-Ender who had been a journalist and an editor and now had his own show on the radio. Allen Carr was famous for his book and programme, *The Easy Way to Stop Smoking*.

'So, 'ow d'you get into it in the first place?' asked Jameson.

Carr explained that he used to be a heavy smoker and had tried, and failed, to quit many times. In desperation he went to see a hypnotist. At the end of his session he stepped outside and lit a cigarette.

Three days later he was about to light a cigarette and he found himself thinking, 'I don't need this.' He realized that every cigarette he smoked fed the craving for the next one, and he stopped smoking there and then.

Carr thought the hypnotist was, to quote, 'useless'.

I thought he (or she) was a genius.

Not only did they cause Carr to stop smoking *and* make him think it was his own idea, but the suggestion was so powerful that it turned Carr into a man with a mission to stop everyone else smoking too.

In the words of one of my early hypnosis teachers, Stephen Brooks, 'Hypnosis is a way to give people presents without them noticing.'

My first term at university was strange. In the first week I auditioned for a Jacobean tragedy I had never heard of called *The White Devil*. I made it to the second round of auditions and went off for lunch with my fellow hopefuls. Afterwards we drove back to the theatre and someone jumped out of the car to read the cast list. I had been cast as Flamineo.

'Who's he?' I asked.

'He's Bracciano's servant,' came the reply.

Rehearsals took over my life. We had a professional director, Malcolm Edwards, who was inspiring, magical and demanding. One evening we rehearsed a scene over and over and over again but I could not satisfy him. As I walked home I decided I could not do it so I should resign. We had three weeks to go before we opened. As I walked towards the theatre the next day it dawned on me that if I resigned someone else would have an awful lot to learn in the next three weeks.

'Malcolm,' I asked, 'have I got the lead in this play?'

'Yes,' he replied.

'So ... I can't really resign now, can I?'

In performance I had an extraordinary experience. I felt completely aware of myself, completely engaged in the action, and a tangible sense of connection to the audience – and I felt more, so much more, that I cannot put into words. The play was a success.

Later, doing other plays, I began to wonder, 'What happened there? What is this difference between a good and a great performance? How come we can sense it so immediately and yet have so little clarity about what is happening and how it is created?'

Very occasionally I have been in the audience of such a performance. I hope you have too.

In the late 1980s I was standing at a lectern looking a vast, half-empty meeting room in Phoenix, Arizona. I noticed a tremor in my leg and realized, to my amazement, that I had stage fright. Having acted in many, many plays by then I was impressed by my ability to be intimidated.

I was at a conference of the Milton H. Erickson Foundation. Sadly Erickson had passed away by then. He is one of several American heroes I never met.

As I listened to the other presentations it occurred to me that each therapist seemed to have a slightly different understanding of human being. On the one hand that is entirely natural – different people have different opinions – but on the other it was a little strange that the job of all these people was to help human beings, but they did not have a single, central definition of human being. This troubling thought would not go away, and so with the grandiosity of youth I decided to sort it out. I returned to university, some nine years after having left.

I re-started my studies at Warwick University in England. I found congenial accommodation on a barge on the Grand Union canal. I was still living and working as a psychotherapist in London and I had also recently started working with Paul McKenna, who was then a Capital Radio DJ and starting his career as a hypnotist.

Warwick was one of the few universities in the UK which encouraged the study of modern French philosophy and there was excitement and deconstructionism in the air. I was not convinced, but it was a stimulating intellectual challenge to make sense of what was being discussed.

In the evening I would drive to my barge. It would take me half an hour to get a little fire going in the stove to heat the cabin, then I would cook my supper looking over the tranquil water at the ducks and coots and the fields beyond. Some nights I would hear my neighbour playing the melodeon. I bought my coal from a passing barge, one of the few still trading on the canals.

Mid-week I would take the train to London to see my psychotherapy clients. My practice continued to educate me and I had enough success to generate more business and feel I was doing some good.

Late in the evening I would meet Paul at Capital Radio to discuss his shows and edit the tapes we were making to help people reduce stress or stop smoking. We would eat at a late-night Italian restaurant and I would soak up the excitement of Paul's ambitious new career.

Warwick was buzzing with intellectual challenges and arcane scholarship. Canal life was quiet, natural and contemplative. My therapy practice was enlightening and sometimes I felt I could be helpful. Paul's world was one of ambition, money and celebrity.

I realized I felt equally at home in each of these four different lives. I could have stopped in any one of them and said, '*This* is the real me.'

Four lifestyles, plus all the travelling every week, was interesting but unsustainable. Through a friend of my father I was introduced to Alfons Grieder, a Swiss philosopher at City University, London. Alfons had studied under Hans-Georg Gadamer, who in turn had been a pupil of Martin Heidegger, whose early thinking was the starting point of my research. I moved to City University, London, and Alfons became my PhD supervisor.

I worked mostly in the old British Library Reading Room in the centre of the British Museum. For six months I gave myself a headache every day struggling to understand Heidegger's *Being and Time*.

Heidegger took issue with the entirety of Western philosophy. He believed that ever since Plato we have overlooked the question of being.

'What,' you could reasonably ask, 'is the question of being?'

Heidegger meant that we do not have a good answer to the question: 'What is being?'

However, as he immediately points out, we must have *some* understanding of being because we use the word 'is' – the third person singular form of the verb 'to be' – to ask the question.

That's philosophy: even a simple question gets complicated. Hence the headache.

Although Heidegger was as pernickety as other philosophers, his understanding was very different. A typical analytic philosopher might state, 'This is a table,' and ask, 'How do we know that statement is true?' and then pose questions about knowledge, perception, truth conditions, verification and so on.

Heidegger's approach was rather to ask,

'Hey, hey, hey! How come I *already know* this is a table? I *must* know it is a table because I have been using it for the last half hour!'

He is pointing out something so immediate and straightforward that most philosophers totally overlook it. He points out that the basic way we meet the world is we make use of it.

When I go to make a cup of tea I don't open the kitchen door and perceive a rigid horizontal surface extended in space below and in front of my feet and subsequently interpret it as 'the floor'. I just walk in. The floor to me is 'for walking on'. Similarly the kettle is 'for boiling water' and the mug 'for holding tea'.

Heidegger asserts that the *being* of things is a function of our purposes. And here we are at the edge of a very deep, dark forest of philosophizing. We are not going in. Let's just extract two ideas:

First, the ordinary, everyday way we meet things is that we use them.

Secondly, it follows that understanding is built-in to our perception. We know what things are because we know what they are for.

Imagine we meet in the street. I am parked by the kerb and you are walking past.

'Hey, Hugh,' you say. 'What's that in the back of your car?'

'Oh that?' I reply. 'It's a rectangular plastic casing with some pipes, fans and little electric motors inside.'

'OK, smart guy,' you say. 'What *is* it?'

'It's an aircon unit.'

'Thanks.'

My first answer was accurate, detailed and unsatisfactory.

The second was sufficient because you know what the thing is when you know what it is for.

While I was PhD-ing I was continuing to work as a hypnotherapist. A fashion arose of using stories during trances as a mode of indirect suggestion. The idea was that if you had a client with blonde hair you could make up a story about a princess with blonde hair. It sounded clunky to me. But I had just met a woman who was a storyteller so I went to her workshop to find out how professional tellers did it.

Storytellers have no script. They see the story in their mind and tell what they see.

Imagine I ask you what you did last weekend and you tell me.

Half an hour later a friend asks you, 'What did you do last weekend?'

You will tell the same thing to your friend as you told me but you do not repeat exactly the same words. That is how the oral tradition works.

I loved it.

Soon I started to get gigs as a storyteller, and soon after that I started my own venues, booking myself and other storytellers. The more I listened to stories and told stories, the more I found stories popping up in my therapy work, not in the cringey, copycat way but unexpectedly and miraculously.

After a particularly painful consultation I told a client a little story about a polar bear, really just a joke, to lighten the mood.

The next week, as she walked in she said, 'I know why you told me that story. It kept me going all week.'

She was holding down a steady job working for a dentist but I remember making a passing remark that she was the kind of person who could go to university. She was bright.

A week or two later she brought in a large bag of pills that she had been saving up to kill herself. She asked me to keep them for her. I agreed, on the condition that she could have them back as soon as she asked. She never asked.

After a few more sessions she left.

Six months later she sent me a neatly written letter telling me that people like me should never be allowed to mess with people's heads and if she had enough money she would sue me.

I put the letter on her file.

Eighteen months later I received another letter. She had just completed her foundation year at university and was writing to thank me because: 'If it hadn't been for you, I would never have got here.'

I put the letter on her file.

2
ORALITY

In 1996 Carl Sagan was interviewed on television. He observed,

> 'We've arranged a society based on science and technology, in which nobody understands anything about science and technology. And this combustible mixture of ignorance and power, sooner or later, is going to blow up in our faces. Who is running the science and technology in a democracy if the people don't know anything about it? [...] Science is more than a body of knowledge, it's a way of thinking. A way of sceptically interrogating the universe with a fine understanding of human fallibility. If we are not able to ask sceptical questions, to interrogate those who tell us that something is true, to be sceptical of those in authority, then we're up for grabs for the next charlatan, political or religious, who comes ambling along.'

People used to ask me, 'What are your clients like? Do you get to see really crazy people?'

'My clients,' I would reply, 'are people.' Pause. 'Just like you.'

I saw all sorts of people. I saw millionaires and models and one woman who spent her entire disposable income on her sessions with me. All of them taught me something.

We all have feelings we can't control and don't understand, we have decisions to make with incomplete information, and often what we think we know turns out to be wrong.

It's not easy.

At my gigs I told stories from the oral tradition. Before there was writing, almost every society had stories that were told over and over again. As literacy spread, the habit of storytelling faded. Fortunately many folklorists collected traditional stories and wrote them down. Collections such as *Grimms' Fairy Tales* and *The Arabian Nights* are famous worldwide.

Grimms' Fairy Tales are rather unsatisfying to read. Characters appear simple. The action seems so often to be similar – beautiful princess, three brothers, impossible challenges, ogres, mountains, oceans, stepmothers and so on and on. Reading a traditional story is like looking at the score of a symphony. It is not very entertaining. The symphony doesn't happen until an orchestra plays it.

To tell a story well you have to get it off the paper and bring it back to life. How do we do that? Here is an opportunity for a long, interesting and enriching diversion. We will not take that diversion here because, if you think about it, it would be a rather strange thing to do in a book. We can do it better when we meet.

Instead, let's do a little thought experiment.

Imagine you hear a story. Why would you bother to retell it? There must be something about that story that you value enough to go to the bother of telling it to someone else. And why would they retell it? Again, there must be something about it they like enough to want to share it. Before stories could be written down they only survived by being retold, so lots of people must have felt like retelling them.

Every traditional story is like a pebble on a beach, washed by a thousand waves of telling, and each teller felt something, maybe the same or maybe different, or maybe they all felt the same thing in a different way. We have no way of knowing. All that we can know is that every traditional tale must have something in it that somehow sings to humanity.

There wasn't really a plan to my storytelling, apart from hoping to entertain people. I just used to tell stories I liked; a few that I had heard from others, many that I read and resuscitated and gradually a few anecdotes of my own. In the British Library I found a marvellous Soviet collection from Siberia with several stories I loved and still tell to this day. I mislaid the name. The book must still be in there somewhere, on the long, silent miles of shelving, but I have not managed to find it again.

In those early years of therapy a brave young man came to see me. He was masturbating up to four times a day. This was long before masturbation became a liberal pastime or a fashionable renunciation. He just wanted to stop. He had already waited for months for, and then seen for months, a clinical psychologist, to no effect.

He told me he had two fantasies: one involved women's clothing and the other I have forgotten, but it was equally unremarkable. I put it to him that he had a third fantasy which was to have a satisfying, long-term, heterosexual relationship. He blushed and agreed. I was very proud of my 'third fantasy' idea.

In the next session I found myself telling him about a time from my schooldays when a monk, a teacher, had told us that during the holidays he had been to the United States and there he had fallen in love. Yet here he was, back at school for the next term, still faithful to his vow of celibacy.

The following session my client told me he had stopped masturbating.

He didn't refer to my third fantasy or to hypnosis or the other fancy Ericksonian interventions I had created. He told me it was the story of the monk that made the difference to him.

I was slowly seduced by the British Library. A repository of all the printed books of the United Kingdom and a great many more from elsewhere, it is a slow-motion, algorithm-free version of Google Scholar. I found myself following footnotes and from those I would follow more footnotes and so on and on into deep, deep thickets of learning.

My interest in storytelling became entangled with my philosophical quest. I researched the oral tradition and soon I came across Walter Ong. Ong was a Jesuit priest and professor at St Louis University, Missouri, who spent his career exploring 'orality' – the term he coined for the way of thinking of people before literacy.

I had stumbled into a vast new world of scholarship. An early explorer of that world was Milman Parry, a brilliant young Harvard scholar who was found shot dead in a hotel room in Los Angeles on 3 December 1935. He was 33 years old.

Before his untimely death he had revolutionized classical studies by demonstrating that Homer, the world-famous author of the *Iliad* and the *Odyssey*, was not the world-famous author of the *Iliad* and the *Odyssey*.

Parry showed that the texts that have been handed down to us as 'Homer's' are actually transcriptions of extemporized oral performances.

Homer's poetry is built with pre-fabricated phrases that fit the metre of the poem. Parry hypothesized that these units of description and action were used because each telling was improvised afresh.

The teller, or perhaps singer, of the tale used a repetitive rhythmic pattern: in the *Iliad* a dactylic hexameter, three syllables repeated six times. He would pick a phrase to fit the requirements of the metre as his telling unfolded. 'Bold Achilles' when he need four syllables, 'Golden-hair'd Achilles' for six and so on.

Parry vindicated his hypothesis by travelling to Yugoslavia with his student, Albert Lord, and recording non-literate tellers of epic tales. Just like the unknown bard transcribed by Homer, they too used formulaic expressions to fit their metre, in their case of ten syllables. Parry and Lord recorded them and verified that the tellers did not have a memorized script. Each performance was an improvisation in which they used phrases of the right length and stress to fit the metre of their poems as they unfolded.

I spent months wandering in the Narnian wardrobe of orality. If you wish to explore it too, Albert Lord's book *The Singer of Tales* and Walter Ong's *Orality and Literacy* are wonderful introductions. We will return to their work, but we don't have time to go on a long excursion now. We must press on.

Milman Parry's work influenced Eric Havelock, a British citizen who built his professional career in North America. He was a professor in Toronto, then Harvard University and later Yale and, like Parry, advanced a revolutionary idea.

Havelock proposed that Plato's philosophy was driven by the impact of literacy on Greek thinking. In *Preface to Plato* (1963), Havelock goes into complex arguments and highly detailed analysis to advance his claim. Many of his peers rejected his thesis and philosophers ignored it.

I did not ignore it at all. I had just plunged into the world of oral storytelling and I was intrigued.

Plato is not complimentary about writing. In his *Seventh Letter* he states he would never put his best ideas into writing because when they are read he would not be there to defend them.

It is strange, isn't it, that Western philosophy is built on the writings of a man who himself declares that they are not his best ideas?

In the *Phaedrus*, Plato tells us a curious story:

> When Thoth invented writing he took it to Thamus, King of Egypt, to distribute to his subjects. Thamus said to Thoth,
>
> 'Those who acquire [writing skills] will cease to exercise their memory and become forgetful; they will rely on writing to bring things to their remembrance by external signs instead of on their own internal resources. What you have discovered is a receipt for recollection, not for memory.
>
> 'And as for wisdom, your pupils will have the reputation for it without the reality: they will receive a quantity of information without proper instruction, and in consequence be thought very knowledgeable when they are for the most part quite ignorant.
>
> 'And because they are filled with the conceit of wisdom instead of real wisdom, they will be a burden to society.'

The *Phaedrus* dates from around 370 BC but the story is older, probably much older. Given the presence of a god you may consider it to be fictional. On the other hand, as a prophecy it is stunningly accurate. It is not at all difficult to look around the world today and see people who are 'filled with the conceit of wisdom' and 'a burden to society'.

Plato doesn't tell us what happens after Thamus' speech. However, we can make a pretty good guess.

I guess Thoth was annoyed by the criticism. As a god he could not go back on his word, but I suspect that he did not give to Thamus the gift he originally intended for him. Instead, I believe he gave him one of his earlier versions of writing, the pictographic hieroglyphs we know from Egyptian archaeology. In a pictographic alphabet the word for a tree is a stylized picture of a tree. Each new thing requires a new icon, which makes a pictographic alphabet very clunky.

I think Thoth kept back his best version of writing. Eventually he decided to try again and hawked it around other Mediterranean nations. In what is now Lebanon he found the Phoenicians, a nation of traders, and to them he gave his best version, the phonetic alphabet.

A phonetic alphabet is like the one I am using right now. Letters stand for sounds, not things, so with around thirty letters you can write any word that can be spoken. You don't need to create and learn thousands upon thousands of symbols. A phonetic alphabet is more efficient, more flexible and easier to learn than a pictographic one.

Historians date the first Phoenician alphabet to around 1050 BC. The Phoenicians traded with peoples all around the Eastern Mediterranean. It is thought they brought the alphabet to the Greeks around 800 BC.

Havelock's *Preface to Plato* is still in print and it is fascinating but not an easy read. His argument about the impact of literacy is complicated. I am greatly indebted to Havelock but I have a simpler version. It is best approached through a question:

'What is a word?'

This is not a trick question. I just want you to think about how you would answer that question. Pause for a moment, stop reading, and decide your own answer.

When you have done so, read on.

So, what is a word? Very often people answer by pointing to a word, for example like **this**, and say, 'That's a word.'

Another common reply is something like, 'It is a collection of symbols that carry a particular meaning.'

These are good answers. They are not wrong. However, I would like you to consider this: the most essential form of a word is a *sound*. Long before we had writing, people spoke to each other. They made sounds. When we talk now we still make sounds. Even when we write or read texts such as this, we make sense of the writing by understanding the sound it represents, even if we only make the sounds in our imagination.

The basic form of language is sound and in fact, as Albert Lord discovered, even our modern notion of 'a word' is a consequence of literacy:

> When asked what a word is, [the story singer] will reply that he does not know, or he will give a sound group which may vary in length from what we call a word to an entire line of poetry, or even an entire song. The word for 'word' means an 'utterance'.

The primary form of a word is not a set of letters on a page. Words are sounds and sounds are *events*.

'Well, so what?' you might ask.

Well, as it turns out, so quite a lot.

Writing made life much, much easier, but also indirectly more difficult.

There is a haiku by Matsuo Bashō painted on the window of the café in which I am working today:

Sitting quietly doing nothing

Spring comes,
And the grass grows by itself.

I ask myself,
'Does this haiku belong
in the jigsaw of this book?'

We tend to assume that a written sentence is the same as a spoken one. We don't make a big deal of it, we just assume that in most situations writing and speaking are the same. Often we even use the word 'saying' to mean 'writing', as in, 'What do the instructions say?' Or, 'In the Bible it says ...'

Imagine you say to me, 'Hey, Hugh, I'm really looking forward to reading your book,' and I write it down, just like that.

Your spoken words vanished as soon as they were spoken. However, you can re-read what I have written as often as you wish. I don't have to write it again. It is still here. It will still be here if you read this tomorrow. It is not eternal, but it will exist for as long as there is a copy, somewhere, in some form, of this writing in existence. The same is true for every written sentence in the world. Words that were only spoken are gone for ever.

This is the first consequence of writing: **written words have fixity.**

For too many people, this consequence is painful right now. The net is a junkyard of indefinitely preserved gossip and casual commentary. Your career could be ended because of some careless remark typed years ago.

The second difference between orality and literacy is that **written words lack emotional inflection.** Every spoken word has some kind of tone which conveys the speaker's feelings. Before writing there could be no unemotional verbal messaging. Even now when people try to speak 'unemotionally' they convey an emotional message which is something like: 'I do not wish to engage with you,' or 'I will treat you as an item, not a human being.'

Because the written word has no emotional tone it diminishes the transmission and salience of feeling. Of course skilful writers of novels, poems and plays – and personal letters, and blog posts and emails and so on – can convey very powerful emotions. But it requires a certain skill or a certain authenticity to convey emotions accurately on paper. We are not all great artists.

The reduction of emotional expression is thoroughly normal. Writing offers us a subtle encouragement to reduce our immediately expressed and experienced feeling. The upside of this is vast. Writing allows the unemotional recording, preservation and transmission of facts.

What could possibly go wrong?

The third consequence of writing is more difficult to understand but bear with me. It is worth making the effort.

Writing permits and encourages *a new way of thinking.*

Consider this: I am writing these words in a café in Saigon, Vietnam. Now, as you read them, they have been transported away from the café in which they were created. You could be reading them anywhere, at any time in the future. In this most simple sense these words have been abstracted – taken out – from the place they originated.

In an exclusively oral world you can't do that. In the oral world meaning *happens* when we speak and then recurs only when we recollect it in memory.

The situation changes with writing. As written words persist, so too does their meaning.

The meaning of a written word doesn't exist like a stone or a chair or a telephone. The meaning of this word, 'chair', is not a specific chair, nor is it inside a chair, nor in my head, nor yours, nor is it floating around the coffee machine.

It is not 'inside' the words or the sentence. It is more like a shadow or a virtual image. It exists in some non-physical way. Meaning becomes an *abstraction*. It is almost as though there is some special realm somewhere beyond actual things and words by means of which we understand the text 'chair' and what it refers to.

We have just reproduced an approximate version of one of the earliest and most famous philosophical theories: Plato's 'Theory of Forms'. We have also, in a very crude way, reproduced Eric Havelock's argument that Plato's thinking was affected by literacy.

Put simply: **writing facilitates abstraction.**

Nowadays we can talk about the meaning of words and the definition of words separately from the words themselves. We can point at a piece of text, or hear an audio recording and ask, 'What does that word mean?'

In a pre-literate world that distinction, although possible in principle, would be extraordinarily difficult to think about or use. The very notion of a definition arises from literacy. There are no dictionaries in an oral culture. The act of speaking was an expression of meaning and meaning didn't exist unless it was being expressed.

It is right about *now* that I would expect your eyes to glaze over. Time for a break.

In ancient times there was a great destruction and all living creatures had perished save one man. He was called Markandeya and he was walking without stopping through the desolate landscape. There were ruins and mud and pools of filthy water. There was no life anywhere. He walked and walked and all of a sudden he stopped and turned around. Behind him there was a tree, a green, living tree. He walked towards it and he saw a young boy sitting at the foot of the tree.

The boy said to him, 'You look tired. Come.'

The boy's mouth opened wide, a great wind arose and Markandeya found himself lifted up into the air and blown down into the boy's mouth and further down and down and down until he found himself deposited in a beautiful green meadow. Around him there were cows grazing. A group of girls were chatting and laughing as they carried water to their village. Markandeya followed them and was kindly greeted and fed. He walked on through that country, through villages, towns and forests. He went down to sea and he climbed up great mountains. For seven years he explored that marvellous land and then one day a great wind arose and he found himself lifted up into the air and he went up and up and up until he found himself blown out of the boy's mouth and standing once more in front of the tree.

The boy smiled at him and said, 'I hope you are well rested.'

That story is from the great Indian oral epic *The Mahabharata*.

I heard a friend tell that story and at the end she said, 'And the moral of the story is ...'

It took me several years to forget whatever she said next.

I have two very strict rules when I am teaching storytelling: no titles and no morals.

To sum up so far, literacy facilitates three phenomena:

- Written words, and hence their meaning, persist over time.
- Writing allows us to state things with little or no emotional expression.
- Writing encourages us to think abstractions.

Writing has made possible amazing advances of art and culture. It is the basis for all technological progress. Few people have seriously considered that it may also cause a few difficulties.

Remember Jay Haley and 'I'd never let that be the problem'?

We cannot know exactly what he thought but we can note that 'symbiotically attached' is a diagnosis founded in a literacy-based thinking. It describes a state rather than a process and it utilizes a theory to describe emotions – in short, it exemplifies fixity, abstraction and lack of emotion.

I suspect Haley thought that the diagnosis 'symbiotically attached' was not the most helpful route to resolving the problem.

After about four years of studying part-time for my PhD I was ready to give up. I had wandered far from my original ideas and along the way I had mislaid my sense of purpose. I didn't feel that my original research question was adequate. I went to see my supervisor Alfons in his small, tall office in Northampton Square and opened by telling him that I wanted to change the title and topic of my thesis.

'Splendid,' he said. 'Your thinking has developed. That is a good sign.'

I tried again. 'Alfons, there's another thing. I really don't want to read any more boring books.'

'Yes,' he replied, 'that is a good strategy. Don't waste time. There are already enough good books. Don't read the boring ones.'

I carried on.

I completed my PhD 1997. I didn't achieve my grand definition of human being. My interests in philosophy, storytelling and therapy had unexpectedly come together in my thesis and my final achievement was an elucidation of the significance of oral storytelling in performance and psychotherapy.

I was delighted to finish. I didn't realize that I hadn't finished at all. The enquiry I had started would stalk me for decades.

I continued to be confused about being a philosopher. I was inspired by the insights of great thinkers, I had met a few truly fine enquiring minds and I still found myself haunted by deep and awkward questions, yet academia seemed too distant from real life.

Over time I came to realize that I am not drawn to philosophy as it is currently defined:

> 'The study of the fundamental nature of knowledge, reality, and existence, especially when considered as an academic discipline.' Dictionary.com

> 'The study of general and fundamental questions, such as those about reason, existence, knowledge, values, mind and language.' Wikipedia

The original meaning of 'philosophy' is built into the word: in Greek, *philo* means 'love of' and *sophos* means 'wisdom'. In the modern definition, wisdom appears to have gone missing.

I am interested in original philosophy.

3

WHAT IS THIS?

One sunny afternoon I was riding my motorcycle. The bike was capable of more than 140mph but on this occasion I was riding at about ten miles an hour because I was on a narrow, deep, twisty, country lane. I braked as I met a car coming the other way. My front wheel ran on to a patch of gravel no bigger than the palm of my hand. The bike skidded and fell and I went over the handlebars and dislocated my collarbone.

We were right outside a friend's house, so my friend looked after the bike. The driver of the car was taking his wife to work at the local hospital so they gave me a lift to A&E.

It didn't really hurt and I was fine until the man in the cubicle next door started to explain to the nurse how he had been drilling through a piece of wood balanced on his knees and the drill had gone through... The blood drained from my head. At that point my girlfriend arrived. It took a while to reassure her I was fine.

After I had recovered from the bruising and my shoulder was working again, I was shocked to discover that I could no longer do a simple press-up. To restore my shoulder and keep a basic level of fitness I decided to do some yoga. Not three classes a week. Not an hour a day. My goal was just five minutes of yoga, a few 'salutes to the sun', five days a week.

I missed many days, but usually this very, very small target was achievable. I would get out of bed, have a shower and do my five minutes before getting dressed for the day.

Sometimes my five minutes would expand to ten or even twelve minutes. It became part of my morning routine for more than ten years. Yet more often than not I would be standing in the shower and find myself thinking, 'Oh I don't need to do it today. I have so much to do. It is just a hassle. My work is more important. That yoga doesn't matter, I need to check my emails.'

Even though I already knew that every time I do my yoga I appreciate it, I still heard this self-important voice in my head saying, 'I don't need to waste my time on that.'

As that little voice kept on and on, day after day, year after year, it raised a question in me. Where does that voice come from? After years of doing something that is free and healthy and enjoyable, why do I still repeatedly have a thought telling me not to do it?

So now alongside my unsatisfied philosophical musings I had another nagging, strange question:

'How come I can continue to have such foolish thoughts in my head when I know at every level that they are absurd?'

In 2020 the lockdown madness hit us. My son's school closed, my morning routine was disrupted, and even though I had more free time at home than ever, that foolish nagging little voice seized the moment and took over.

My five minutes of yoga disappeared. My years and years of repetition counted for nothing. My tiny little island of healthiness sank into an ocean of distraction.

After the lockdowns ended my yoga didn't just pop up again. It has taken another *year* to get it back. I am forced to admit that that nagging, lazy, self-important voice is one of the strongest forces in my psyche.

So now my nagging question is worse:

'How come I can continue to have such foolish thoughts in my head when I know at every level that they are absurd, and how come those thoughts are so persistent and powerful?'

Am I just lazy? But even if I am lazy (OK, I am), is that really an explanation, or is it just a label? Why am I so consistently tempted to be lazy when the action I desire is so manifestly rewarding? That's not just lazy it is foolish.

I was doing some research on behalf of the UK government's Department for Culture Media and Sport. I was talking to a group of regular gamblers in Walsall. They were a friendly gang and explained how much more fun it was to watch a game when you had some money riding on it.

One of them had had a few drinks before our discussion.

'You gotta know your limits,' he explained. 'Wiv gamblin' you gotta know your limits. I know my limits, I do. Fing is, when I get there, I don't always stop.'

Why do we not do things we want to do?

Equally, why do we do things we don't want to do?

Why don't people who want to lose weight just eat less?

Why don't smokers and drinkers and gamblers just stop when they want to stop?

We love to imagine that we run our own lives, but to do so we have to ignore all the evidence that we don't.

What is wrong with us?

Let's pause for a moment.

So far we have some stories, some anecdotes from psychotherapy, some fragments of philosophy and some thoughts about the impact of writing. Now all of a sudden we find a discussion of the author's willpower and human fallibility in general. Isn't this a bit messy? Are there not too many topics in this book?

In fact, what sort of a book is this?

A collection of short stories?

An autobiography?

Popular psychology?

Popular philosophy?

An analysis of human frailty?

A puzzle book?

Entertainment?

Self-importance?

Self-help?

And given my obvious interest in philosophy, and the fact that I already have a PhD which is a kind of passport to academic credibility, why am I not writing a proper academic book?

That is already a good set of questions – but there are more:

Who is this book for?

And *what* is it for?

Does it have a message? A purpose? A use?

How can we answer all of these questions?

It is very tempting to answer one question first, 'What sort of a book is this?' because the answer will tell us in which category the book belongs, and that will answer a lot more questions.

When you walk into a bookshop you will find books grouped by category, each with its own heading: Fiction, Biography, History, Philosophy, Travel, Psychology, Economics, Self-Help and so on. If we know the category, we know what to expect. So, for example, if this is a collection of short stories we can expect:

- o The stories are probably fictional.
- o I may be moved but I am not expected to think hard.
- o The overall purpose is entertainment with perhaps a touch of enlightenment about the human condition.

If, however, this is a self-help book we can expect:

- o Guidance.
- o Exercises.
- o Encouragement.
- o The possibility of achieving a real improvement in our real lives.

This use of categories, or headings, is a very ordinary way of organizing books, and things in general, even our thoughts. In fact it is so ordinary that it is no more remarkable than drinking a cup of tea.

However, according to Walter Ong, when Pierre de la Ramée first proposed it in 1543 it was a revolutionary new mode of thinking.

This technique of headings is made possible by pen and paper. You can write a heading and add items beneath it one at a time, and keep it available without an effort of memory. You can write another heading for another set of items.

Under each heading you can create subheadings and under them further subheadings and so on. You can create different groups or classes, you can highlight similarities or differences and so on. A cloud of random phenomena can be organized neatly under headings.

In principle you could do this sort of analysis without writing but it is much easier on paper. You can also marshal arguments by itemizing points for and against, and you can build arguments by a sequence of such oppositions. Classifying thoughts under headings like this became known as Ramism, and it was the predecessor of dialectical argument taken up by Hegel.

Whoa!

We are steering towards the deep, dark forests of philosophy again. Dear reader, you have gotten this far and I don't want to lose you now. We are *not* going to talk about Hegel. He makes Cerberus look like the Andrex puppy. If you don't believe me, have a look at *The Phenomenology of Spirit*. Open it anywhere. Any page will do. If you want to stay sane, close it again.

All I want to note now is that headings create categories by means of one or more shared characteristics.

Categories are a type of *abstraction* facilitated by literacy.

Did you notice what happened just there?

First, we did not answer all those questions. We began to answer one of them and veered off. That's the sort of thing that happens all the time in everyday conversations, but the rational, organized writer tries to avoid doing it. A rational approach raises a topic, addresses it and moves on. It doesn't leave ragged, unanswered questions ...

Secondly, we illustrated a simple, everyday way in which we use abstractions to make life easier. Abstract categories like this are all over our lives. When we know what sort of book this is we know how to treat it. We already have expectations of each type of book so we know where it fits – or doesn't – in our lives.

If you pay close attention you can notice a feeling a bit like relief when you say to yourself, 'Oh, it's one of *those* books.'

Conversely it is a bit unsettling if the book doesn't fit in a category.

The upside of knowing the category of book is that we have some idea what to expect. The downside is that our attitude to the category may cause us to prejudge the book:

'Philosophy books are boring.'

'Self-help books don't work for me.'

'I don't like short stories.'

Insert your own belief or prejudice here ...

Now let's be kind to that rational part of the mind and try to answer those questions.

Q. Hugh, what sort of a book is this?

A. That's difficult. It is a semi-biographical, impressionist, puzzle portal to a new yet ancient paradigm of cognition. Writing it is like fumbling for stepping stones in a sea of philosophical quicksand. It is practical, original philosophy. It is a bunch of stories. It is all of the above and more, and less.

Q. Isn't that a bit messy?

A. Yes. A bit like life. Of course, a part of me yearns to be able to put things into categories with a nice logical order. That is the academic side of my thinking. But if I try to offer a fully explicated and referenced text I would hardly get started before I ran out of time and long before that almost all my readers would leave me to live a less painful life. Another part of me just wants to tell you more stories about how I got here and what I glimpsed on the way. This part is acutely sensitive to how boring theories can be and how much they cannot capture. There is something absolutely vital in stories that cannot be captured in theory or explanation.

Q. Is this popular philosophy?

A. I hope so! Well, at least I hope it is popular, but this is not academic philosophy. Readers acquainted with philosophy will notice that I am dodging massive, intractable, ancient and ongoing philosophical discussions on pretty much every page. However, in the old sense, yes, this is real philosophy. It is written from a yearning for wisdom. We may never know if we achieve it, but it is a noble goal.

Q. Is this popular psychology?

A. Again, I hope it is popular, but I am not popularizing academic psychology. There is plenty of good work out there already. One of the many plagues of modernity is that there are simply too many books. Now there are also too many videos and online courses and blogs and explanations and commentaries and summaries and so on and on. We don't need another 'me too' introduction to psychology. Nonetheless I have learned a great deal from my psychotherapy clients, so I hope to share some of that with you.

Q. Is this a puzzle book?

A. Yes, in a way it is. It is almost a detective story. When it started I didn't realize what was going on, any more than you. I just had a nagging question about theatre and then a nagging question about therapy. Gradually I was dragged into the philosophical forest and by the mysterious workings of fate I found a path which took me to the study of orality and then back to philosophy and psychotherapy and storytelling, and eventually to an understanding of understanding.

Q. Is this an autobiography?

A. I tell you about me because my life is what I have available. I am retracing my journey so that you may see some things of interest. And, ticking off two more questions, yes it is an analysis of human frailty, and an exercise in self-importance. It would be false modesty to say I'm not special. But it would be equally wrong to say you are not special. We all have unique possibilities and we are all going to die so let's make the most of them before we go.

As for whether this could be entertainment or self-help: well, I hope to be entertaining and helpful from time to time.

Q. Why am I not writing a standard academic book?

A. There are lots of very good reasons for that. I am not trying to build a career in academia, so I don't have to publish to get my next job. I'm writing for everyone, not just academics. Furthermore if I tried to write 'proper' philosophy it would take for ever. I've been there. My PhD took seven years and that is only the tiniest beginning of the understanding I am writing about today and hardly anyone has read it. In academic publishing I would never get far enough to point towards the stuff that is really important. Even worse, all my readers would have to study philosophy to understand the philosophical jargon and arguments I would be required to use. Sadly, progress in academia is very slow. Martin Heidegger died in 1976 but he never completed the project he outlined in *Being and Time* in 1927.

Finally:

Q. Who is this book for?

A. You. And all your friends. And anyone who is a little bit dissatisfied with what normality offers these days.

Q. And what is it for? Does it have a message? A purpose? A use?

A. These are all the same question. Yes, it does have a message and a purpose and a use. If I could sum it up in one sentence here I would. But I can't. That's why I need a whole blinking book. And when you get it, and I really hope you do get it, you will understand how much more there is that can't be caught in a book.

I have told some stories, thrown out some questions and opinions and claimed that literacy introduces three tendencies:

- Fixed meanings.
- Loss of emotional tonality.
- Abstract thinking.

My claim is that these phenomena are just tendencies. They are not irresistible forces or unstoppable causes. The invention of literacy didn't force anything to happen. It just enhanced certain possibilities which have had a huge impact on being human.

We have also touched on the difficulties of being human, and we will explore those issues further a bit later on. Let us stay, for the moment, with literacy and its children.

Historically the impact of literacy was limited until the advent of the printing press in 15th-century Europe. Up to that point Europe was dominated by the Catholic Church. Martin Luther and others rebelled against that domination and the new technology of printing let them distribute their ideas quickly, accurately and cheaply all over Europe. They brought about two centuries of conflict and creativity.

Today we are at the beginning of a similar upheaval. The transformative technology is the internet. Like printing, the internet delivers phenomenal, world-altering benefits and subtle distortions. Just as Europe was once flooded with pamphlets of competing ideas, today powerful forces are struggling to harness the internet for their purposes.

The internet presents another fascinating diversion and although it is super important I will not take it. I have written a little elsewhere about the internet, and many others have investigated its perils, but there is far, far more yet to be explored. However, I must finish this expedition before starting another. Here let us note just these points:

- The internet perpetuates and amplifies all of the impacts on cognition of literacy: abstraction, fixity and lack of emotional subtlety.
- The worldwide web delivers instant worldwide communication but it is usually edited, and even when live it is constrained by the viewpoint of the camera and the lack of embodied sensitivity. It would perhaps be better named the world thin web.
- Mobile access to the internet changes, we could even say distorts, the context in which we live and hence our sense of proportion. That which is distant, yet edited, can jump out of our phone and into our heads. With our heads full of messages and imagery designed to catch and trap our attention, there is less room for the less vivid yet more rewarding challenges of our immediate lives.
- The internet augments the pressures and distortions which we saw first with the impact of its predecessor, the television. Jerry Mander was one of the first to realize how profound and significant were the changes induced

by television. Two decades later Robert Putnam's research detailed the social consequences.

- o The internet amplifies conflicts and extreme points of view and under-represents the centre. It allows people to be physically separated and yet more emotionally dependent. It delivers astonishing transactional efficiency, and *efficiency* comes to dominate much of its content in the competition for eyeballs, just as it did on television earlier. And to what end is the net efficient? As ever the most immediate and simple end comes to dominate: money.
- o Centralization and gigantism are hugely facilitated by the internet, so small human-sized businesses with human-sized jobs are driven out by hyper-efficient systems which replace mundane yet fulfilling local jobs.

Jerry Mander was a partner in the most successful advertising agency in California in the 1960s. When he tried to use his expertise to promote an eco-friendly initiative and failed, he began to question the nature of television and gradually came to see it as a destructive force. As he observed some years before the internet came into our lives:

> This society upholds a fierce technological idealism. We believe we can get the best from a given technology without falling into worst-case scenarios ... [however] ... most technologies are actually deployed in the manner that is most useful to the institutions that gain from their use; this may have nothing to do with public or planetary good.

Modern science, medicine and culture are founded in literacy. Facts can be recorded, data can be shared, ideas can be transmitted. Literacy is the first technology. It is the foundation for all other technologies and hence the foundation of modern, developed civilizations.

Look around you now. Unless you are sitting alone in a forest or desert or some other wilderness, you are surrounded by things that have been made with technology which was made possible by literacy.

The benefits of literacy are so prolific as to be uncountable. Literacy makes all these benefits possible because:

- Abstraction facilitates analysis and theorizing.
- Removing emotional tonality promotes objectivity.
- Fixity of meaning enables the precise transmission of data.

There is a long and enthusiastic celebration of the world-changing achievements of literate cultures all around the world. I too celebrate the wonders of technological progress. There are many books for which I am extremely grateful. I have benefited enormously from the fabulous labour-saving technologies of our age, from a literacy-based education and the preservation of knowledge and stories.

Nevertheless I suggest that alongside these magnificent, world-changing benefits, literacy has indirectly helped us to make terrible mistakes and very slowly and indirectly it has fostered dangerous misunderstandings because:

- Abstraction tends to reduce the significance of context.
- Removing emotional tonality tends to reduce subtlety of understanding.
- Fixity of meaning tends to lead to cognitive inertia.

It is not that simple. You may have noticed that 'literacy' is itself an abstraction. Literacy is not at all uniform. Its quality varies from sublime to appalling. There is good writing and there is bad writing and there is disagreement about what counts as good or bad. The good bits can be very good indeed, but they are rare, and difficult to achieve. If something reads well, someone worked very hard to make it so.

Writing must be cogent and coherent to deliver a lucid message regardless of context. Writing forces us to think more clearly. We cannot divert, retrace or correct ourselves as we do in conversation. We do not receive the non-verbal clues of the live listener to inform us that our meaning is being conveyed. We must deliver self-contained clarity, but at the same time strive to be concise and elegant in order to retain the reader's attention.

The reward of learning to write well is that it teaches us to think well too. As we reread and reflect upon the written sentence, much of the time we realize it is inadequate or inaccurate. It must be rewritten. An idea that could be carried in conversation, in context, with feeling, must be wrought and polished to become robust on paper, and in that process of refinement we find its flaws and are forced to work on it further. Often we must pull back from too grandiose a claim; occasionally we find a deeper, richer insight beneath our initial observation.

Prolixity, pedantry and platitudes perpetually seek to insinuate themselves in every line to dull our wits and anaesthetize our readers into boredom. Writing is an astonishingly demanding discipline which schools me to this day.

We can compare literacy to a tool, such as a knife. It can be used well or badly; to do good or evil.

At its best, literacy and the thinking and analysis it makes possible have elevated the human spirit, enriched our understanding and civilized our world.

At its worst, the consequences of literacy are banal, malign and destructive of our environment, our society and our souls.

As we shall see later, I suggest that literacy is often best used when supported by learning from other modes of education.

Perhaps this book is like a chocolate cake. The fact that you can't eat it all at once doesn't make it a bad cake. The better the cake, the more slowly you want to eat it. If it is a really good, rich chocolate cake you might want to eat just one slice and come back later for more.

4

KANT OR SOLOMON?

Before we disappear into a cloud of conceptual analysis, let's ask a couple of basic questions:

> Is this proposal even true? In other words, did literacy *really* change thinking?
>
> If it did, given the overwhelming benefits of literacy, what, if anything, is the problem?

The easiest way to answer the first question is to look at what life is like without literacy. We compare a literate society with a non-literate society and itemize the differences.

Unfortunately that is not easy at all. There are almost no societies left in the entire globe that have not been affected to some extent by literacy.

A hundred years ago more people were still unaffected by literacy. In 1925 Carl Jung was travelling in New Mexico and met some Native Americans. He noted, 'The Pueblo Indians derive consciousness from the intensity of feeling. Abstract thought does not exist for them ... They cannot go beyond the perceptions of their senses and their feelings.'

One particular conversation with a chief called Ochwiay Biano struck him so powerfully that he remembered it ever after. He wrote it down many years later in his autobiographical *Memories, Dreams, Reflections*:

> 'See,' Ochwiay Biano said, 'the whites always want something; they are always uneasy and restless. We do not know what they want. We do not understand them. We think that they are mad.'
>
> I asked him why he thought the whites were all mad.
>
> 'They say that they think with their heads,' he replied.
>
> 'Why of course. What do you think with?' I asked him in surprise.
>
> 'We think here,' he said, indicating his heart.

Walter Ong's research was focused on the nature of orality rather than the impact of literacy, but his copious research is revelatory. His exploration of historical records uncovered overwhelming evidence of the differences between literacy and orality-based thinking. Once again I must fight off the tendency to divert into a summary of his work. Walter Ong died in 2003, another great American I never met.

Ong's work pointed me towards Alexander Luria, who was a Soviet scientist, later better known for his work in neuropsychology. In the 1930s Luria conducted research among pre-literate peoples in Uzbekistan and Kirghizia.

Luria's aim was not to investigate orality per se but 'the study of how self-consciousness is shaped in the course of human social activity'. However, his report beautifully illustrates orality-based thinking. He tried to get non-literate people to think in terms of abstract categories. He failed, repeatedly. For example, he asked his respondents to consider a group of four things – saw, hammer, log and hatchet – and asked them to name the odd one out.

The reply that almost all literate people will give is 'log' because the other three are tools and the log is raw material.

Luria's illiterates resolutely refused to do that. They believed that the tools and the log belong together. The hatchet splits the log and the saw cuts it up. Many said they would take the hammer out, because although it is useful to knock the hatchet they could manage without it. Even when the researchers pointed out that saw, hammer and hatchet are all tools and the log is not, their suggestions were rejected:

'Yes, but even if we have tools, we still need wood – otherwise we can't build anything.'

'If you get rid of the log, what good would the others be?'

Luria reported, '... we had no luck in getting these subjects to perform the abstract act of classification. ... they operated on the basis of "practical utility", grouping objects in practical schemes rather than categorizing them. When we referred to a generic term they could use to designate a distinct group of objects, they generally disregarded the information or considered it immaterial.'

Luria gives many detailed examples of how his illiterate subjects responded to his experiments. When, for example, a researcher showed a picture of three adults and one child and said, 'Clearly the child doesn't belong in this group,' the reply was as follows:

'Oh but the boy must stay with the others! All three of them are working, you see, and if they have to keep running out to fetch things, they'll never get the job done, but the boy can do the running for them ... The boy will learn; that'll be better, then they'll all be able to work well together.'

Luria's respondents were intelligent and capable but they actively rejected abstraction. They consistently used the real world and their own practical experience to make sense of his questions.

Luria wrote, 'The semantic and psychological structure of this [illiterate] mode of thinking is unique. Words have entirely different functions than they do in a system of abstract thought; they are not used to codify objects in conceptual schemes but to establish the practical interrelationship of those objects.'

Luria summed up his fieldwork as follows:

> Their thinking was wholly unlike that of subjects trained to perform theoretical operations. Our subjects used concrete, 'situational' thinking to compile groups that were extremely resistant to change. When we tried to suggest another group (based on abstract principles), they generally rejected it, insisting that such an arrangement did not reflect the intrinsic relationships among the objects, that a person who adopted it was 'stupid' or 'did not understand anything'.

In 2007 Daniel Everett published *Don't Sleep, There Are Snakes*. Everett spent the greater part of thirty years living with the non-literate Pirahã in the Amazonian jungle. I heartily recommend his book to find out why he was there and what happened. His research focused on linguistics rather than literacy, but his findings provide more insights into orality-based thinking. Everett was puzzled for years by many aspects of the Pirahã language and the world view it entailed. Some things just didn't make sense to him. One puzzle was cleared up when he came to realize that the Pirahã don't discuss anything that they have not witnessed or was not witnessed by someone they have met.

Everett called this the principle of immediacy of experience. Everett's principle was paralleled in Luria's work seventy years earlier in Uzbekistan. For many of Luria's respondents, personal experience placed an absolute limit on what could be meaningfully discussed: 'The subject refused to discuss any topics that went beyond his personal experience, insisting that "one could speak only of what one had seen"'.

A further significant consequence of the principle of immediacy of experience is that it precludes talking in abstractions:

> [The principle of immediacy of experience] would explain the lack of numerals and counting in Pirahã, because these are skills that are mainly applied in generalizations beyond immediate experience. Numbers and counting are by definition abstractions, because they entail classifying objects in general terms. Since abstractions that extend beyond experience could violate the cultural immediacy of experience principle ... these would be prohibited in the language.

When Everett writes that abstractions would be 'prohibited', he implies there are 'rules of the language', which of course are an analytic construct posited post-hoc by linguists such as himself. The Pirahã themselves have no such rules, of course, because rules are abstractions. They just don't talk like that.

Everett realized that language and world view and lives of the Pirahã people are organized by the principle of utility. In his words, 'The Pirahãs are firmly committed to the pragmatic concept of utility. They don't believe in a heaven above us, or a hell below us, or that any abstract cause is worth dying for. ... They have no craving for truth as a transcendental reality. Indeed the concept has no place in their values. Truth to the Pirahãs is catching a fish, rowing a canoe, laughing with your children, loving your brother, dying of malaria.'

You may remember that Martin Heidegger claimed that Western philosophy since Plato – that is, according to Havelock, since the impact of literacy – has lost its way and overlooks the fact that the primary way in which we meet objects in the world is that we *use* them.

There is a whole library of historical evidence of the difference between orality and literacy-based thinking and there are thousands of books and papers debating the minutiae of the details. There are far more differences between orality and literacy than I touch on here.

The key point is that there is massive historical and contemporary evidence that oral societies rarely if ever engage with abstractions. So the answer to the first question,

'Did literacy *really* change our thinking?' is:

'Yes, literacy *really did* change our thinking.'

Is this a bit intense? When I'm telling stories there is always a time when everyone needs a break. We need to get up, stretch our legs, let the stories sink in. Maybe have a drink. We tend to forget we can do that when we are reading a book because the eye naturally runs ahead and books, like TV programmes, are often written in such a way as to keep you engaged.

I would rather you had a chance to rest and digest. Consider this paragraph an interval. See you soon.

What about the second question?

Given the overwhelming benefits of literacy, what, if anything, is the problem?

If there are problems, we can suggest two things:

First, they are as tightly woven into the fabric of our societies as literacy itself and hence could be, and probably are, all around us all the time.

Secondly, whatever these problems may be, we have lived with them for a long time. Writing was originally a technology for the rich, powerful and religious. Then, with the advent of printing in the 15th century, both texts and readers multiplied rapidly as reading and writing spread outside the privileged classes. By the end of the 18th century approximately half the population of Europe could read. So if, simplistically, the problems are proportionate to the number of literates, they will have accelerated in the 15th century, and again, more rapidly, since the 18th century. We will find that is the case, but I'm running ahead of myself.

Let's pause for a moment in the 18th century, the century of the Enlightenment, perhaps the first European high-water mark of literacy, a massive expansion of study and knowledge hailed as the triumph of reason over ignorance.

A central figure of Enlightenment thinking was the philosopher Immanuel Kant. He was famous for seeking a rational foundation for morality. In his day Reason was the Great New Hope, rather as Science is – or was – now. In both cases the Great New Hope was destined to deliver rather less than was desired. A central element of Kant's moral philosophy was his Categorical Imperative: '*Act* only according to that maxim whereby you can, at the same time, will that it should become a universal *law*.'

This is perhaps the ultimate moral abstraction.

At first glance it sounds admirable. Is it not a fine goal to do that which is always necessarily right? With a little more thought we can see it is absurd. If the decree is as vague as 'Be kind', the categorical imperative tells us no more than the initial injunction. If the action is more specifically designated, we can ask how could I have time to consider all possible variations of a situation and devise an action that would be appropriate in all of them? Furthermore, his proposed law is impossibly grandiose. There are no two situations that are identical. Any action repeated regardless of context is necessarily less than wise.

Our societies are built on literacy. If there are problems arising from literacy they should show up very frequently indeed. They should be visible all around us every day – and indeed they are but these problems are so ordinary and we are so used finding more superficial reasons for them that we mostly fail to understand them.

Out of billions of possible examples here are just two well-documented events from the 21st century that illustrate the problems arising from our tendencies towards cognitive inertia, reduced emotional understanding and abstraction. Let us look at a tragedy from 2015 and a farce from 2019.

Tragedy

On 24 March 2015 Andreas Lubitz flew a Germanwings Airbus 320 into a French mountain and killed all one hundred and fifty people on board. Lubitz was depressed and suicidal.

The prosecutor appointed by the French government asserted that doctors had told him Lubitz should not have been flying, but medical confidentiality requirements prevented his physician from making this information available to his employer.

Under German law, employers do not have access to employees' medical records, so employers must rely on employees to declare their lack of work fitness.

Every commercial flight has at least two pilots. So why didn't the other pilot, in this case Captain Patrick Sondenheimer, stop Lubitz? When Sondenheimer left the cockpit to go to the toilet, Lubitz locked the cockpit door. Sondenheimer was unable to break in because in the aftermath of the hijacking of four airliners on 11 September 2001, aviation authorities had mandated that all cockpit doors should be reinforced to prevent unauthorized entry.

The primary cause of the death of Andreas Lubitz and one hundred and forty-nine other souls was Lubitz's murderous suicide.

Lubitz's action was facilitated by three policies:

> Medical confidentiality: Lubitz's doctor was prevented from giving any warning to Germanwings by the policy of medical confidentiality.
>
> Legal prevention of access to the medical records of employees: Germanwings were unable to monitor Lubitz's (or any other employee's) mental health by the law (a legally enforced policy) preventing them from accessing their employees' medical records.
>
> Impregnable cockpit doors: Mandated by aviation authorities worldwide post 9/11.

From tragedy, let us turn to farce.

Farce

In 2019 Harry Miller was told by the Humberside Police that some tweets he forwarded would be recorded as a 'non-crime hate incident'. Harry realized that 'recording a non-crime hate incident' was an infringement of his rights. It was also an overreach of police powers, it had potential for unjust consequences, and it was a waste of time, money and police resources.

He took the Humberside Police to the High Court and won; then, in the Court of Appeal, he took on the College of Policing, who had issued the original guidance, and won against them too.

Harry told this story in a panel discussion hosted by the Free Speech Union:

> Following my High Court victory I had a sit-down meeting with the Chief Constable of Humberside and I said to him, 'Look, I kind of understand why an enthusiastic young officer came off a course and got it entirely wrong. What don't understand is why somebody up the chain of command didn't apply some common sense.'
>
> ... The Chief Constable looked me in the eye and said, 'Harry, what you must understand is that common sense is not an appropriate tool for a police officer because it leads to unpredictable outcomes. What we need is more guidance.'

The Chief Constable, a Mr Lee Freeman, preferred to place his faith in abstract 'guidance' rather than address the specific details of a particular event. This is the essence of Kantian folly. Common sense is sensitive to context, proportion and human behaviour, as well as to 'guidance', and it is precisely what we should wish for to generate sensible outcomes, even if they are unpredictable.

The job of a leader such as a chief constable is to use his authority to ensure that his subordinates do the best job possible, and they do not merely follow guidance. If guidance were all that was necessary, we would not need leaders. It follows from his own words that Mr Freeman is redundant. But perhaps I am too harsh.

Mr Freeman is probably a very nice man. He is, according to his biography, a football coach and a cyclist. Everyday life, rife as it is with unpredictable outcomes, must be torture for him, and he must have been severely traumatized as a child when he realized the existential burden implicit in his surname. Perhaps he should change his name to Mr Lee Guidanceman.

What has this to do with literacy? With writing one can specify requirements precisely and permanently. Literacy makes possible policy-making. Kant's maxim, the Categorical Imperative, is the grandfather of policy-making. All policies are instances of Kant's Categorical Imperative: '*Act* only according to that maxim whereby you can, at the same time, will that it should become a universal *law*.'

Policies are **abstractions**. Policies which mandate actions necessarily cannot make provision for unknown subsequent changes. Hence, sooner or later, all policies, without exception, fail, because any action repeated regardless of context is necessarily less than wise. In Lubitz's case the failure was tragic. The murders were directly facilitated by a policy specifically intended to save lives.

'Oh, come on,' you may riposte. 'It is unfortunate, but we cannot rid the world of homicidal lunatics. There is nothing we could have done.'

But things could have been different. Before the policies that facilitated Lubitz's murder-suicide were introduced (each one designed for the benefit respectively of patients, employees and passengers), a doctor worried about the suicidal ideation of a pilot would have been able to call the pilot's employer to raise his concerns; access to Lubitz's records, or a phone call to his previous employers, would have revealed his prior treatment for psychotic depression and suicidal ideation; a locked but not reinforced cockpit door could have been breached.

Furthermore, the hazard was foreseen. My own brother, for example, a commercial pilot at the time, wrote to his Flight Operations Director warning that the fortified cockpit door policy 'will end in tears'.

Risk, like lunacy, cannot be eliminated.

The alternative to these inadequate policies is not another policy. A better response than increased policy-making is to trust responsible people to find the best solutions available to them in each context. We won't all be right all the time, but we will tend to make better decisions than passively following inadequate policies.

Following policies creates habits of disempowerment.

Making decisions creates a habit of making decisions.

Sharing the experience of decisions made by individuals creates a repository of wisdom to inform ongoing decision-making. You could even call it storytelling ...

And what could Mr Freeman have done differently?

Let's go back to around 900 BC. King Solomon had to make a difficult decision. Two women laid claim to a single baby. One claimed the other had stolen her son.

'Cut the baby in half!' decreed Solomon.

The woman whose son was alive was deeply moved out of love for her son and said to the king, 'Please, my lord, give her the living baby! Don't kill him!'

But the other said, 'Neither I nor you shall have him. Cut him in two!'

Then the king gave his ruling: 'Give the living baby to the first woman. Do not kill him; she is his mother.'

Note that King Solomon's wisdom did not establish a fact. There is a possibility, in spite of the King's word (and the Bible's), that the woman to whom he gave the baby was not his real mother.

However, his judgement was *wise* because she was definitely the one who cared most for the baby's welfare.

Solomon did not have a policy of bisecting babies. Nor did he 'will that it should become a universal *law*'. He understood how people react and his intervention forced the revelation of the most loving woman.

The judgement of Solomon is such a famous story that it has become a byword for wisdom. Ah, how much trouble would have been saved if Chief Constable Freeman had used his judgement.

So, it seems that the answer to the second question – 'Given the overwhelming benefits of literacy, what, if anything, is the problem?' – is as follows:

The problem is that literacy introduces tendencies to take abstractions more seriously than reality, to induce cognitive inertia and to bypass the development of emotional understanding.

Some people, in some circumstances, mistake their understanding of abstractions for an understanding of the real world.

Which doesn't sound too bad until you realize the consequences.

Time to pause again.

It seems I am now claiming that every policy will in due course become inadequate because:

- It is limited by the understanding of those drafting the policy.

- Once a policy is in place, it will eventually be gamed by malefactors just as Lubitz gamed the security of the cockpit door to kill people.
- The world changes in unpredictable ways.

Fair enough, some policies turn out to be inadequate. But policies are all around us. Corporations, governments, universities, charities and institutions of all kinds create new policies all the time. Safety experts can produce evidence that policies have saved hundreds of thousands of lives.

I have already indicated that being human is not easy. What is wrong with policies that make our lives safer and easier?

Am I seriously condemning them all?

Yes indeed I am, and absolutely No, not at all.

Policies are not necessarily destructive. Quite the opposite. Many policies – for a random example banning the use of lead in potable water pipes – are life-savers.

The problem with policies is how we use them.

Policies can *help* us make decisions. They are dangerous if they *replace* us making decisions.

Sticking with aviation a little longer, safety in the air has been greatly enhanced by the policy of using checklists at designated stages before take-off. Before every take-off, every pilot goes through a specific protocol for his aircraft to check that the control systems and engines are functioning correctly.

However, the ultimate decision as to what to do at any point is always made not by the checklist but by the captain of the plane.

An everyday example of another safe and efficient policy is the designation of the side of the road upon which to drive. In the UK, people drive on the left-hand side of the road. Occasionally, for example while overtaking or avoiding a hazard, we divert from that policy for good reason.

Policies can be useful tools, socially and individually. They are a poor substitute for personal authority and decision-making. Ultimately you are in the best position to make decisions about your life, even though some of your decisions will be wrong.

After I left university for the first time I worked for almost a year at a theatre on the outskirts of London, then I joined a troupe of actors to take our own productions to the Edinburgh Festival. One piece was to be a stage adaptation of a radio play; the other was a new play which I had started, but not finished, writing.

As rehearsals proceeded the radio adaptation went well enough but it became clear that my play needed more work. The actors became frustrated. I struggled. The script and the staging were not even adequate, let alone exciting.

For ten nights before we were due to travel to Edinburgh I lay awake all night, terrified, cold and sweating. I discovered that the cliché 'a cold sweat' is an accurate description of a real phenomenon.

In Edinburgh and in desperation we continued to rehearse. I asked Malcolm Edwards, by then a good friend, to help. He walked into the rehearsal room, looked around, paused and remarked, 'I have never walked in to such an atmosphere of hatred in my life.'

Even Malcolm could not help. The radio adaptation played its run. After one performance of my play to half a dozen people in a vast and expensive auditorium, the rest of the company disappeared and left me and Edinburgh and a considerable debt.

What went wrong? I did not have enough experience as a writer to understand how much more work was necessary to turn a 'good idea' into a workable script. I did not have enough experience as a director to patch up the mess I had created. But perhaps my greatest folly was that I believed that if you start a job, you should finish it, and that it was wrong to quit when things were going badly.

It was obvious for several weeks before we got to Edinburgh that my play was in trouble but I lacked the insight and humility to realize I was not capable of rescuing it.

I was following a *policy*, an internalized imperative to finish what I had started, which blinded me to the reality of the unfixable problem I had created. You could say I was hypnotized.

I should have given up earlier. I should have stopped, apologized to my fellow actors, and reduced my losses as much as possible.

I should have quit.

My sad little tale complicates matters. Life would be simple if we could say, 'Those policy-makers, those bureaucrats are to blame! Sack them all and everything will be better!'

But my experience shows that we can internalize policies and make bad decisions all on our own. I made my own mistakes. It wasn't anyone else's fault. I had installed a policy in my head and was brushing aside all the evidence that I was wrong.

If internalized policies create problems, why would I suggest that making our own decisions will generate better outcomes than following public policies?

What if an awful lot of people make decisions as bad as mine?

On the other hand, why do policy-makers claim that they make better decisions than other people? They presumably have some expertise in order to become policy-makers, but is it the right sort of expertise? And what happens if they make *worse* decisions than other people?

In *The Wisdom of Crowds* James Surowiecki collected evidence that teams of experts easily make mistakes. This may appear counter-intuitive, but someone recognized by their peers as an expert must, by definition, tend towards orthodoxy within their field. Orthodoxy creates blind spots because it is necessarily constituted by fixed ideas in a changing world. Academics are a particularly error-prone type of expert as they tend to know too much about their own speciality, not enough about the whole field, and even less about the limitations of how their field connects to the real world.

Surowiecki reported that the decision-making of groups of experts was *improved* by the addition of non-experts.

James Surowiecki's main thesis outlined the conditions in which groups of people, however large, are most likely to make good decisions. Individuals in the groups should be diverse, decentralized and independent. A decision should be made by each person individually and the output aggregated.

It is worth noting that social media do exactly the opposite. They amplify homogeneous, extremist groups, inhibit independent thinking, centralize opinion, stigmatize deviation from orthodoxy and facilitate conflict rather than aggregation.

The net makes us a very unwise crowd indeed.

Perhaps now you are glimpsing the outrageousness of my claims. I have outlined three tendencies and a few illustrations. The scope of my illustrations to date compared to the implications of my claim is like pointing at two Brazilian ants and saying we are looking at part of the Amazon rainforest. They are a very, very small part of the Amazon rainforest.

Is this perhaps a friendly chat about the end of Western civilization? Where else could we look for evidence? Politics? Education? The politics of education? The target set by the intellectual yet idiotic Mr Blair in 1999 to get 50 per cent of young adults into higher education? The department of education? Any department of government? Any government? Any university? Any institution?

This claim about literacy cuts across and beneath entire fields of scholarship that are hundreds of years old. Almost every academic in every department at every university in the world could find an argument to disagree, diminish, dismiss or divert from this claim.

I am pointing out some tendencies. Not *irrefutable causes,* not *universal consequences,* just *tendencies.*

Even worse than Martin Heidegger's admonishment of the entirety of Western philosophy since Plato, my basic claim is appallingly simple.

That is embarrassing.

It is so embarrassing that legions of academics will not even reject it. They will turn their backs and refuse to discuss it.

Politicians will ignore it.

What happens next is, as ever, up to you.

I was talking to a friend about a book I had read and he said, 'I've never read a book.'

He is a successful international businessman.

I was very surprised – and I thought of all the joy and illumination I had received from books. I picked up my copy of *Don't Sleep, There Are Snakes* and lent it to him. It is wonderful, but it has nerdy sections so perhaps is not the most welcoming to be the first book you ever read. A couple of weeks later I asked for it back because I was using it writing this.

He had not finished it but he gave it straight back to me. He told me he was enjoying it. A few weeks later he left the country. Later he told me that he bought his own copy in order to finish reading it.

I miss my books.

I sold my home in London during lockdown so I was unable to visit and take away my favourite books before everything went into storage.

I like books.

I have written books.

For twenty-five years I have been aware of the irony of writing about the limitations of writing.

Daniel Everett came to realize that the Pirahãs benefited from the absence of abstraction. He observed that, though their life was harsh, they had contentment and happiness.

He writes, 'I have never heard a Pirahã say that he or she is worried. In fact, so far as I can tell, the Pirahãs have no word for worry in their language.'

Everett felt that the Pirahã were in many ways better off than 'advanced' societies.

Is there something beneficial about oral societies that has been lost by many people today?

Pre-literate societies are universally poor, lack technology and know very little about the outside world. Surely I am not advocating we return to a pre-industrial lifestyle?

No, I am not.

My point is not so extreme. I concede immediately that the three tendencies have made possible countless benefits. My point is that they have also made possible many disbenefits which are not understood.

Here is an analogy. There is a bug in our thinking software. It is not like a bug in a program. It is like a bug in the language in which all our programs are written. And that language is the language we have to use to debug ourselves.

My intention is not to lay waste to literate culture. Far from it. I would like to *rescue* it.

The most important question now is not, 'Are my extraordinary claims about the impact of literacy justifiable?'

You can look around your own life and see the evidence everywhere, although I do concede that there are none so blind as those who will not see.

A more important question to ask is, 'How is it that some people or organizations *do not* make errors founded in abstraction, inertia and insensitivity?'

How do some people get the best of literacy and avoid the disbenefits?

How do some people – some modern, literate people – understand more clearly?

5

A LADDER

A young woman had a dream. In her dream she saw a beautiful head-dress, a wreath of gold and silver leaves beaten so fine that they shivered in the breeze.

When she woke she ran to her father, the king, and said, 'Daddy, Daddy, I just had a wonderful dream. I saw a head-dress, a wreath of gold and silver leaves beaten so fine that they shivered in the breeze.'

'If you dreamt it, you shall have it,' said her father, and he summoned all the goldsmiths and silversmiths in the land and commanded every one of them to make a head-dress, a wreath of gold and silver leaves beaten so fine that they shivered in the breeze.

'The one who makes the head-dress that my daughter picks shall win his weight in gold,' proclaimed the king.

The day came when all the silversmiths and goldsmiths brought their wreaths to the king's great hall. The wreaths were placed on four long tables and by each one stood its maker.

The king's daughter came in, fizzing with excitement. She made her way along the first table, the second, the third, and as she reached the end of the fourth table she burst into tears.

'It's not here!' she cried and she ran out of the hall.

She ran down the steps, across the courtyard, out of the gate, through the town and out in the fields. She ran and she ran and she ran. She ran into the forest and through the birch trees until her tears were dry and she could not run any more.

She was in a little clearing, a tiny patch of blue sky above her, silver grey trunks and pale green leaves all around her.

She saw a flash of brilliant white – and there, coming through the trees towards her was a huge white bear. Between his two front paws the bear was tossing a gold and silver wreath, a wreath of gold and silver leaves beaten so fine that they shivered in the breeze ...

'Oh, please, please, please,' begged the king's daughter, 'give me that wreath!'

'You may have the wreath,' said the bear, 'if I can have you.'

'Anything!' said the girl hastily, and she took the wreath and she walked and skipped and ran all the way back to her father's palace.

The next Thursday, the king, her father, ordered the palace gates to be locked and the palace guard to be doubled. The bear came out of the forest, across the fields, through the town and up to the palace gate.

He knocked the gate down and swiped away the guards as though they were skittles.

He walked across the courtyard, up the steps and into the great hall. There was the king with his three daughters.

'I have come for your daughter,' said the bear.

The king did not want to lose his youngest, precious daughter. He pushed forward his eldest daughter.

'You go,' he said.

The girl climbed on the back of the bear, and the bear turned and walked out of the hall, down the steps, across the courtyard, out into the town and as he reached the fields he began to run and as he did so he spoke to the girl on his back and he said,

'Have you ever sat so soft? Have you ever seen so clearly?'

And the girl replied,

'Yes, I sat this soft on my mother's lap. I saw this clearly on my father's knee.'

The bear reared up. The girl fell from his back.

'You are not the one!' he roared.

And the girl ran, terrified, all the way back to her father.

The next Thursday, the bear came again. The king had repaired and reinforced the gate and tripled the guard.

The bear smashed the gate as though it was an eggshell. He brushed off the guards like ants. He walked across the courtyard and up the steps and into the hall and he said to the king,

'I have come for your daughter.'

And the king, who did not want to lose his youngest, precious daughter, pushed forward his second daughter and he said, 'You go.'

And the girl climbed on to the back of the bear. The bear turned, went out of the hall, down the steps across the courtyard, out of the broken gate, through the town and as he reached the fields he started to run and he said to the girl,

'Have you ever sat so soft? Have you ever seen so clearly?'

And the girl replied,

'Yes, on my mother's lap I sat this soft. On my father's knee, I saw this clearly.'

The bear reared up and girl slid from his back.

'You are not the one,' he roared.

And he snapped his great jaws at the girl and she ran terrified all the way back to her father.

The next Thursday the gate was stronger than ever, all the king's guardsmen were on duty but it was no good. The bear broke the gate like a twig and he swatted the guards like flies.

He walked across the courtyard, up the steps, into the hall and he said to the king,

'I have come for your daughter.'

The king looked at his youngest daughter.

She climbed on the back of the bear, he turned and went out of the hall, down the steps, across the courtyard, out of the broken gate into the town and when he reached the fields he began running and he said to the girl on his back,

'Have you ever sat so soft? Have you ever seen so clearly?'

'No,' she said and her eyes were shining, 'Never have I sat so soft. Never have I seen so clearly.'

'You are the one,' said the bear and he ran on.

The girl held on to his deep, soft, snow-white coat and the bear ran and ran and ran and he ran on to a great and marvellous story that is far older than this book and far, far beyond it.

You can read the bones of that story in a wonderful collection by Abjørnsen and Moe but if you are curious, if you keep asking and if you are fortunate, one day you will meet a real storyteller, and you can say, 'Please tell me the story of the white bear.'

And perhaps you may *hear* the rest of the story.

Back in 2003 I wrote *How to Mend Your Broken Heart* with Paul McKenna. It took us two years. We talked and thought and discussed and planned and started writing, then it fell to pieces. We started again and again. We tried so many different ways. There was so much work, so much rewriting and editing and revision and re-revision. When it finally came together it felt like a miracle. All that work paid off. We are very proud of that book and it has helped many, many people, but it was hard, exhausting work and it felt so disorganized.

My next book was about negotiation. I was determined that it would be different. I had a commission and a deadline. I conducted my research then I sat down, I drew up my plan and I dutifully wrote five thousand words a week.

It was like drowning in a marsh of treacle. The more I wrote the more depressed I became. After six weeks of writing I was horribly bored. If I was bored writing it, how would my readers feel?

I did the obvious thing and ran away. I found a ridiculously cheap flight to Mexico leaving the next day from Manchester. I was in London. I booked the ticket and half an hour later my back went into spasm.

The following morning I had to get up at 3am to drive to Manchester. I couldn't stand up. I crawled into the shower and the hot water eased my back. I decided that if I could get to the car I would go. I made it to the airport and had to lean on the counter as I checked in.

I begged the check-in woman to put me next to any empty seat on the plane.

She did, and I managed a sort of curled-up half-lying position.

When the stewardess came round with hot towels I put mine straight on my back.

'If there are any left over,' I asked, 'please could I have them?'

Five minutes later she returned with a trayful.

I put them on my back four or five at a time. The relief was blissful.

As I lay there, deliriously comfortable, I realized what was wrong with my book. I had interviewed some very successful negotiators. They had done deals with ships and cars and houses and aeroplanes. They had brokered deals in union meetings and at market stalls. They had hustled aircraft spares in Africa and oil tankers in Moscow. They were truly remarkable people and each one of them was fascinating.

That was my epiphany. I had been dutifully writing a book about how to negotiate which was pretty much the same as every other book about negotiation, when the really interesting, valuable book was hiding under my nose. The real gold dust was the personalities of these negotiators.

Of course, I had to give my readers the skills and tools of negotiation, but the key was their personal qualities. My interviewees were all curious, confident, flexible, powerful and solution-focused. They were great storytellers and much, much more.

They had the same tools as everyone else, but they were successful because of *who they were*. The real value I could offer was to show my readers how to develop in themselves the personal characteristics of successful negotiators.

Once again I had been led astray by an *abstraction*, an idea about what I should do, the 'sensible' way to write a book. Luckily on this occasion I paid attention to my feelings. I found the answer I needed in my *experience* of the fascination and inspiration I felt as I talked to those great negotiators.

I drew on my skills and experience in psychotherapy and personal change and devised a programme to help my readers develop the required aspects of their personalities.

I rewrote the entire book in ten days on the shores of the Caribbean. I wrote on my balcony every morning with sea sparkling through the palm trees. In afternoons I walked along the white sand beach and swam in the turquoise water. I flew back to England and triumphantly produced my manuscript two days early.

'Oh,' said my editor. 'I wasn't expecting you to deliver on time.'

In his deeply unconventional study of being, Heidegger understands humans as 'being-with'. In his words, 'The possibility of transposing ourselves into [other human beings] … already and originally belongs to man's own essence. Insofar as human beings exist at all, they already find themselves transposed in their existence into other human beings, even if there are factically no other human beings in the vicinity.'

Later on we will approach this notion via a different route which explains why he makes this claim. For now, to put it in more everyday (and inexact) language, the claim is roughly this: we are not essentially individuals who can forget ourselves in the herd, we are essentially a herd that has the possibility of becoming some individuals.

If you point out that each one of us has a separate body, Heidegger's assertion seems bizarre. If on the other hand you pay attention to our behaviour, you can see that maybe he has a point ...

There is another thicket of philosophy here which we will bump into again later, but for the moment, as before, we are going to skirt around it. For now, let's look at what follows if Heidegger is correct. If we are always already together and can become individuals, then there is a possibility that we can become individuals together.

Listening to a well-told story, although we may still be sitting in our chairs, we also see and feel the story – we visualize the villains and heroes, we feel the twists, turns and tension together. If what we are is 'feeling understanding', then what we are is transposed into the story. There is far more to this, but I don't want to geek out in philosophy right now. (If you are really interested, you will find the reference for my thesis in the notes at the back.)

Here I am reminded of two events.

First, my ineffable experience in the theatre when I was a student. I could indeed feel the audience, as well as myself and my character, and perhaps they felt me and the character I played.

Secondly, although months and months of sincere effort had failed to help him, my client was freed from his compulsion when he heard the story of the monk who kept his vow of celibacy.

We could say the story changed him – or we could say in the story he changed himself.

I first met Peter Brook at his theatre, the Bouffes du Nord, in Paris. I talked at him for twenty minutes, then he kindly interrupted me and said, 'It's about to begin.'

We went downstairs and I was seated on a cushion in the very front row. The stage started where my feet finished.

A wondrous performance unfolded in front of me. A flock of birds came on stage, each represented by an actor with a sort of half puppet. Not only could you see the birds utterly birdlike, but each bird – the sparrow, the raven, the hawk, the stork – was definitively recognizable.

The Conference of the Birds is a frame story, a big story with smaller 'pop-up' stories embedded within it. A bird would ask a question and the hoopoe would answer, 'Ah, it is like the story of the sultan and his two daughters.'

And there on the stage would be the sultan and his two daughters. The strange thing was that over and over again I did not see these other actors enter. The set was empty. Two carpets on the floor, one hanging at the rear. There was nothing to hide behind and yet the actors appeared.

I had to force myself to stop watching the action of play in order to see the pop-up actors enter or exit.

When the play finished the Parisian audience spilled out on the stage gesticulating and discussing the play with all the joyous pretentiousness of the French intellectual. In the middle of the crowd stood Peter Brook, a still, short man, unseen by the crowd around him.

'What did you think of the play?' he asked me.

'The audience were a bit noisy ...' I said, meaning really, 'Sacrilegious bastards! Here they are witnessing the theatrical miracle of a lifetime and they just giggle and whisper to each other and, and, and ...'

'There's something for everyone in my plays,' replied Brook, meaning, 'I understand you, you over-enthusiastic, serious young man, but people are of all different sorts, and a good play is for all people.'

The poem on which Brook's play was based was written about eight hundred years ago by a Sufi, Farid ud-Din Attar.

The Sufis have a saying that there is a ladder up to heaven. To reach the rung above, we need a helping hand. However, we cannot leave our own rung unless we help someone up from the rung below.

6
DANCING

The story of Thamus and Thoth made an abiding impression upon me. I grew fond of quoting about people 'filled with the conceit of wisdom' who are 'a burden to society'.

One day I was mulling over the story again:

> ... as for wisdom, your pupils will have the reputation for it without the reality: they will receive a quantity of information without proper instruction, and in consequence be thought very knowledgeable when they are for the most part quite ignorant.

And a question popped into my head that should have arrived much, much earlier.

'What,' I asked myself, 'does Thamus mean by "proper instruction"?'

When Thoth brought writing to Thamus he had only just invented it. So there was nothing like a modern school or university because there was no writing, no textbooks, no canon of academic literature. Not even hand-written manuscripts.

'Proper instruction' could not mean 'going to school'. So if there were no textbooks and no schools, how did people learn?

On a weekend in April 2011 I found myself on the Tweed Run. It was notionally a bicycle ride for charity, in practice an excuse to dress up, show off and have fun. Hundreds of tweed-clad people gathered on the steps of St Paul's Cathedral and set off to ride around central London. I was wearing plus fours and riding a Pashley bicycle. We crossed the Thames and came back. People smiled, laughed and clapped as we rode by. We cycled through Mayfair and stopped for afternoon tea in Lincoln's Inn Fields. It was a splendid, sunny, silly day.

The after-party was in the basement of the Bethnal Green Working Men's Club and for the first time in my life I saw people dancing Lindy Hop. I was seized by an extreme passion to dance like that and two days later I was at a Lindy Hop lesson.

Lindy Hop is a dance form created by Black Americans in Harlem, New York City, in the 1920s. The originators of the dance adapted movements from African and European dance traditions and created their own dance to the swing music of the time. They were creators. They had no teachers. There is a wonderful introduction to that time in Frankie Manning's autobiography, *Frankie Manning: Ambassador of Lindy Hop*. Frankie was another great American hero. As with Milton Erickson, I was sadly too late to the party to meet him.

By the 1950s Lindy Hop had fallen out of fashion although a few enthusiasts kept dancing. A revival of the dance started in the 1980s. By the time I started there were small Lindy scenes growing rapidly all over the world. One of the largest groups of Lindy Hoppers in the world is in South Korea.

I went to classes or dances seven or eight nights a week for the next two years. The scene was super friendly. I travelled to festivals and workshops all over Europe. I absolutely adored dancing Lindy

Hop. I danced and practised and tried to steal fancy moves from YouTube. After about two years I was pretty sure that in another six months or so I would be really, really good.

Then, as my awareness slowly caught up with my enthusiasm, I began to see how very, very bad I was.

It was fascinating, and appalling, to discover how limited was my bodily awareness. I was sure that I was doing a little kick just like my instructor and then on a video I would see how much I was unlike my instructor. Not only was I kicking my foot up where she was keeping her foot down, I did not even realize the difference until I saw the video.

Later on, when I was teaching beginners myself, I discovered how difficult it is to teach dancing. You have to teach what they need to do and stop them doing lots of things that they think are right but don't work, and stop them doing lots of other things they don't even realize they are doing. If you explain too much, people get lost. If you explain too little, they get bad habits. If you focus on one element you must leave out another. Above all, your job is to help them *feel* how the dance works and you can't do that directly. You can just keep pointing until they get it themselves.

I remember being told patiently by one teacher to be more gentle. I did my best, and he told me again. And again. I just didn't understand. I had to get my partner from my right-hand side to over on my left. How was she going to get there if I didn't pull her?

We beginners were all blundering around in the dark.

As I travelled around Europe I was lucky enough to dance with some wonderful partners and have dances I remember to this day. Little by little they helped me to find the secrets of Lindy Hop. I didn't need to pull anyone anywhere. If I want someone to go one way, I prep them in the opposite direction. My partner will compress and release her own muscles to create motive power. My lead is not a pull. It is not a command. It is just an invitation.

I can write all this, you can read it. But if you want to understand you have to dance and you have to feel it – and even that is not as simple as it sounds. As a beginner I was trying so hard I could hardly feel anything. My muscles were so tense I could not feel all the subtle signals I was being given. Other dancers are so soft and floppy that they can't feel anything either. Lindy requires just the right amount of muscle tone – not too much and not too little.

So you get that – and then you discover every partner is different, so you have to adjust. As the wonderful dancer and instructor Sharon Davis put it, 'You start as a beginner. You get to be intermediate. Then, at last, you are advanced. Then you realize you are a beginner.'

As I pondered Thamus' 'proper instruction' I realized that **before writing, people learned through apprenticeship**. Indeed for centuries after schools had been established for monks and accountants and rich people, ordinary people learned their trades through apprenticeship.

In mediaeval times an apprenticeship was a direct, personal relationship between an apprentice and his (it was usually he) master (it was usually a man). The apprentice's work, from day one, contributed to the business. A young person would sign up to work for and learn from a master for a fixed period of time. The training could last as few as three or as many as seven years.

The apprentice would start doing menial and basic tasks and observe the working of the business and the more skilful tasks. Little by little, he would take on more difficult tasks. There was a great deal of repetition and yet also much variation, mostly minor, of materials, weather, context, customers and requirements.

The apprenticeship would be completed when the apprentice made his masterpiece. The masterpiece was a concrete demonstration of its maker's skill. A joiner, for example, would make a cabinet, and present it to the Guild of Master Joiners. The masters would examine the piece closely and if it was of a sufficiently high quality the apprentice would be declared a Master Joiner and thereafter be permitted to set up his own workshop and train his own apprentices.

There are very few such apprenticeships left.

In living memory there were still practical apprenticeships in engineering, mechanics and building trades. Some academics and officials will claim that modern apprenticeships have been improved by increased standardization, certification and classroom-based teaching. Some practising engineers, mechanics and builders will disagree.

There were, and in a few special places there still are, the informal apprenticeships of skills passed from parent to child. In the words of Ernie Lennie, an education coordinator for the Dene Nation in the north of Canada: 'The type of learning we get in school and also on TV is the type of learning where we just sit and absorb. But in family life it's a different kind of learning. Children learn directly from their parents. That is the native way of teaching. Learning has to come from doing, not intellectualizing. A long time ago they only taught people by doing things, but now they just sit and watch TV.'

I asked professional friends about my notion of the importance of apprenticeship. Everyone seemed to have someone who had inspired them and helped them to achieve greater understanding. Among others I asked a lawyer, a civil engineer, a pilot, a nurse and a doctor. They all told me how much they had learned from senior, experienced mentors.

As Professor Dreyfus of the University of California, Berkeley, put it, 'Education at its best must be based on apprenticeship. Even science that starts out teaching rules and techniques ends up with the student as an apprentice in a successful scientist's laboratory ... where worldly expertise is concerned, one can only learn by imitation of the style and day-by-day responses to specific local situations of someone who already has the relevant mastery.'

The consequences of the loss of apprenticeship are spread widely across society. They can be seen vividly, and often tragically, in the changes in medicine in the UK over the last generation.

The training of both nurses and doctors includes a significant element of apprenticeship alongside formal study. Thirty years ago, trainee doctors had approximately 30,000 clinical contact hours in training positions over ten to twelve years. They would frequently be on call in hospitals overnight and then go straight to work the next day.

In 2022, trainee doctors have training positions for eight years and get approximately one-third of the clinical contact hours of their predecessors.

Nurses used to gain a diploma after years of work and instruction, almost all of it on wards. Now trainee nurses get far less experience on the wards. Everyone has lost out, including the nurses themselves. By 2022 more than half (57%) of all nurses were planning on leaving the profession for which they have spent years training.

There is far more wrong with the UK's National Health Service than the decay of the training system. There is too much administration, measurement, centralization, poor-quality research, exploitation by Big Pharma, and too many PFI (Private Finance Initiative) contracts and so on and on. So much is wrong. Yet many of the ailments of the system can be traced back to two related causes. The first is the reduction of on-the-job apprenticeship. The second is the ubiquitous application of centrally determined policies.

An immediate remedy would be to delegate authority in hospitals to hands-on practitioners, away from measurement-driven managers. Administrators need to take to heart Goodhart's law: 'When a measure becomes a target, it ceases to be a good measure.'

Good decisions require agents to wield authority in their own immediate domain. Doctors, nurses and front-line staff may not make perfect decisions every time, but they will make better experience- and context-driven decisions than office-bound policy-makers.

This is not merely my opinion as an outsider. It is widely shared, and despaired of, within the medical profession. Many older nurses left the jobs they loved, fed up with the workload, the paperwork and being told what to do by younger colleagues with MScs but less practical experience. The view of many doctors has been eloquently captured by Seamus O'Mahony in *Can Medicine be Cured?* In the margins of Henry Marsh's meditations on brain surgery, *Do no Harm*, one can sense a lament for the lost ethic of work focused on the care of patients.

These critiques are not unusual but there will be many people outraged at this analysis. They will point out how wonderful are our modern nurses and how hard they work, how dedicated are our doctors, how modern is their training. Indeed, in spite of the failings of the system, there are many wonderful nurses and doctors. There are always wonderful people who thrive and blossom even under the most adverse circumstances. Those wonderful people are not the problem.

Part of the problem is that the middle-rankers, those people who are good and willing but fall short of genius, are inadequately supported. They are also let down by a system which burdens them so much paperwork they have little time left to care for patients.

The greater part of the problem is that the NHS is now a helplessly expanding bureaucracy with a few hospitals and clinics attached.

Well, maybe my critics are right and maybe I am wrong. If I am wrong, I am in extensive company. The research business I ran with my colleague David Corr was commissioned fairly regularly to research health issues. We conducted hundreds of discussion groups in the UK. In the late 1990s, if a member of a group said anything critical about the NHS, the other members would turn on and scold them.

'Our NHS is wonderful,' was the dominant opinion.

Ten years later, if a group member said something critical about the NHS, all the other members of the group would pile in with their own horror stories.

'Our NHS is a mess,' was now dominant.

That's just an anecdote from qualitative research. It's just a story. You can't really argue with a story. It's just a story.

My journey into Lindy Hop was learning by doing. It was a chaotic, fragmentary mash-up of learning through experience and apprenticeship. It was not a real, full-time, focused apprenticeship, but as I learned and watched and imitated and danced with better dancers, I collected little moments of understanding. Many of the best dancers had previously trained their bodies. Some had done martial arts, others ballet or gymnastics. As I stumbled on in my donkey body I was very envious of their training.

I am not a naturally talented dancer. I have friends, and indeed a wife, who have danced far less than me and are far, far better. They have natural grace and rhythm. I lack both so I have to work twice as hard to be half as good.

It seems to me that there is a lot to be gained by learning a skill at which you suck. Go ahead and improve your excellence – let your talent shine – but remember that what comes easily to you does not teach you much. Things that are difficult teach us a lot.

Learning Lindy Hop taught me a great deal more than how to dance. I learned about myself. Dancing will show you all the flaws of your character. If you are clumsy, over-eager and demanding – like me – that will show up in your dancing. If you are a self-centred show-off – like me – that will be revealed as you dazzle your audience and annoy your partner. If you are too eager to please – like me – that also shows up.

To get better, you need to overcome your character flaws. At the same time, the good sides of your character come out. Your wit, your dignity, your tenderness, your warmth – it can all be seen in your dancing.

Before writing we also learned through experience. That seems such an obvious path of learning I should hardly need to mention it. We all have experience every moment of every day so we all learn from it, don't we?

Sadly not.

But why not?

The easiest way not to learn from an experience is to believe that we already know what it could teach us. For some people it is almost a point of honour to know what is going on.

'I'm on top of this,' they confide with a knowing look.

Some people dismiss many points of view without taking the time to consider them. It takes confidence to assert that you don't know what is happening.

Ernest Rossi, Milton Erickson's pupil and editor, once observed Erickson working with a married couple. After a while

Erickson asked the husband to leave the room. He then turned to the wife and asked her, 'How long have you been cheating on your husband?'

After the session Rossi asked Erickson how he knew the woman was cheating.

'I've never seen a woman who sat like that,' replied Erickson, 'who wasn't cheating on her husband. But I am curious to meet one who isn't.'

Even if you do know what is happening, it is a mark of greatness to be open to knowing more.

The third mode of learning – along with apprenticeship and experience – before we had writing was storytelling. And here, ironically, words fail me – or at least written words fail me. Learning from stories is unlike academic learning. It is not rational. It is not sequential. It is not conceptual. It is not even clear what you learn.

If the story is boring and badly told it may teach you nothing at all. If a story is well told it speaks to your heart. One day, in the middle of a performance, as I was telling of the hero leaving the forest and walking towards the mountains, I suddenly realized that his situation was exactly like mine. I was telling the essence of my life at that moment.

For some years I was the artistic director of a playback theatre company. In playback audience members are invited to tell stories. There are only two rules: the story must be true, and it must be from the teller's own life. The actors immediately turn them into theatre. Each show is unique and remarkable.

From time to time, after a particularly moving or uplifting show, someone would ask, 'Is this psychotherapy?'

I would reply, 'Before things were separated into fact and fiction, geography and history, psychology and marketing and education and entertainment and psychotherapy and so on, there was storytelling.'

Even on paper a well-written story can move you, in spite of all the limitations of writing, but what sort of learning is that, to be moved?

Jerry Mander recalled asking John Mohawk, a Seneca native American who was then editor of *Akwesasne Notes*, to tell him some traditional stories. Eventually John consented, but only if Mander turned off the tape recorder.

John explained, 'If you have the machine going, or if you're taking notes, you won't understand the story. It depends on your listening with your heart. That won't come out on a machine.'

That may sound a little fanciful but I have many times been shocked at what is not captured by an audio recording. When doing qualitative research we routinely record interviews and group discussions. We have recordings transcribed so that we have accurate quotations to illustrate our analysis. It is remarkable to find that the sentiments and ideas that you clearly remember understanding during the group or interview are not visible in the transcription. In conversation we often stop as soon as we understand that we are understood, so the sentence ... We move on to the next idea, interrupted as I remember that ... Let me put it this way ... and so on.

There is also a deeper level at which John Mohawk is right. A well-told story is more than a list of events. If a story is moving we feel it, and if it is well told we feel it together. Listening to a person is different from listening to a recording. Our feelings can be exquisite and precise even though we may not be able to articulate them verbally. Feeling can teach us and listening to stories can change our way of being.

From a Heideggerian point of view, feeling together is being together, so the telling and hearing of a story is an event of community.

When I first understood what Thamus meant by 'proper instruction', I entered a long and damaging phase of zealous over-enthusiasm. I was so struck by the distortions created by literacy that I told anyone who would listen all about the disbenefits of literacy at length.

I had found a real unconscious bias. Long before the claims of anti-racists and the dubious, semi-retracted implicit bias test, I had found a real, identifiable, unconscious bias. But it didn't go down well. No one wanted to know about the downsides of literacy.

Instead I elicited incredulity and fierce resistance. Almost everyone immediately told me that not only was literacy the foundation of Western culture but also, and crucially, it had liberated the working classes. I was accused of misunderstanding how much literacy had fostered vital social change.

Others pointed me towards the many brilliant writers over the ages whose prose or poetry is illuminating, heartfelt or uplifting. There is so much great literature. How could I criticize writing, when it is the tool of Shakespeare, of George Orwell, of George Eliot, of T. S. Eliot, of thousands of women and men of genius all around the globe?

Gradually I calmed down and learned to place my observations within a recognition of the broader benefits of literacy. I remembered to acknowledge that the possibilities of literacy are glorious, even though some can lead us astray.

In the field of education eventually I realized that the problem was not so much the dominance of literacy as the absence of the other three modes of learning. We suffer from a lack of *balance*.

A balanced education has four pillars: literacy, storytelling, apprenticeship and experience.

Those among us who make good decisions have had an education, however fragmentary and informal, not just from books, but from apprenticeship and stories and experience.

Those among us who make the worst decisions are those policy-makers who live in a world of theory and analysis, who do not suffer from their own policies and have no idea how little they understand. They lack meaningful experience. They lack emotional understanding. They live in a world of clear and stable abstractions as the real world evolves and changes around them.

The power of the thinking made possible by literacy is stupendous. It can be a force for beneficent progress or it can be a blight. The key is to do literacy-based thinking *well,* and to a great extent that is facilitated by the contextual integrity, emotional understanding and narrative comprehension we gain from a truly balanced education.

The section above is a rather abstract discussion, isn't it? Abstractions about abstractions.

If many of us are off-balance because we have only literacy, then we should find that situations that deliver storytelling, experience and apprenticeship improve our balance. Are there any real-life examples of genuine benefits from this so-called 'balanced education'?

There are 12-step groups all over the world. Initially devised by the founders of Alcoholics Anonymous (AA), the programme has been so effective that people have used the AA template to tackle all sorts of addictions, from shopping to sex, drugs and eating disorders.

12-step programmes are all free, entirely voluntary and self-supporting. Somewhere near you, in a church hall or community centre or in a room above a café, there is probably a 12-step meeting happening today, possibly right now.

A common meeting format is that a person who has had success in staying sober is invited to share their experience, strength and hope – their own story of recovery from active addiction.

Meetings always include a 'sharing' time in which anyone present is invited to speak. Usually they are given a time limit, for example three minutes, and they are free to say whatever they want, provided they don't comment on or give advice to other people. People speak about how they feel and share their stories.

Someone who regularly goes to meetings hears, and tells, a lot of stories. **Storytelling** is a vital part of 12-step recovery.

The 12 steps themselves describe a path of acceptance of the nature of addiction and a route to recovery. These are the first three steps of AA:

> Step 1: We admitted we were powerless over alcohol—that our lives had become unmanageable.
>
> Step 2: Came to believe that a Power greater than ourselves could restore us to sanity.
>
> Step 3: Made a decision to turn our will and our lives over to the care of God as we understood Him.

There are endless 12-step discussions about God which, just like twenty centuries of philosophy, I am going to side-step. I just want to make one observation. Someone who takes these steps is making a statement of humility and of willingness to accept help.

They give up the belief that they already know the solution to their own problems. Humility makes **learning from experience** possible.

Commonly people work the steps with the help of a sponsor. People who have previously worked the steps or reached a later step volunteer to help newcomers and those on earlier steps. The sponsor uses his or her own experience, and the honesty and humility they have achieved, to be a support and resource for their sponsee. The relationship is a form of **apprenticeship**.

So, does it work?

Yes.

The single most effective treatment for alcoholism is the Alcoholics Anonymous 12-step programme. There is less research on the success of the other myriad addictions that people overcome with 12-step programmes, but the fact that there are so many thriving groups suggests that for people willing to take the first step there is something that makes them want to keep coming back.

The first time I induced a hypnotic negative hallucination I didn't know what I was doing, nor how I was doing it.

I was having tea at a large, long table with a group of other schoolboys. Eddie, the head monitor, took advantage of his privileges by smoking a pipe. (It was a long time ago ...)

Somebody swiped his pipe and it was passed from hand to hand beneath the table while he was complaining, 'Come on, chaps. Who's got my pipe?'

The pipe arrived in my hands, and after a little while I brought it out and started slowly smoking it.

'Ask Hugh,' someone called out.

'Hugh,' he said, looking straight at me, 'where is my pipe?'

I looked straight back into his eyes, took a puff and slowly moved the pipe away from my lips.

'I'm sorry, Eddie,' I said, 'I really can't say.'

'Oh come on,' said Eddie and he continued to ask who had it.

We were all amazed, myself included, that Eddie could not see what was right in front of him.

He continued not to see it until I turned it round, held it out to him and said,

'Here it is, Eddie.'

7
BEING

We know a lot about human beings. We know about the circulation of the blood, about muscles and digestion and hormones and neurons and synapses, but we easily misunderstand the significance of all this physiological and observational knowledge. It is rather like reading a workshop manual for a car. We can understand the engine, the fuel system, the brakes, the suspension, the steering and so on, but the manual tells us nothing about *the experience of driving the car.*

The mainstream, objective, scientific understanding of humanity has a similar lack but tends to assume that our experience will be explained by a little more understanding of our brainwaves.

As Heidegger pointed out, scientists are too eager to leap into the virtual world of objectivity. They overlook what all of us can work out from our own existence. Pay attention to your own experience now and you can notice three phenomena.

First, **you are always understanding.** You understand these words as you read them, but you also understand your environment. You see your book, or laptop or phone. You see furniture or fields or windows or whatever is around you wherever you are. You automatically make sense of your situation. There are no patches of unresolved pixels. You may occasionally be mistaken, but nevertheless you always have some understanding of your surroundings.

Secondly, **you always have some mood or other.** It might be flat or bored or a bit puzzled but you always have some feeling, some sense of 'how things are with you'.

Thirdly, **you are always deciding how to be** and what to do. Much of the time our decisions are default decisions such as, 'I will carry on doing what I am doing,' or 'I will do what I usually do,' or 'I will do what everyone else is doing,' or 'I will follow whatever distracts me next.'

However, at any moment I could do something else. I could stand up and shout. I could wave my arms. I could buy a ticket to Buenos Aires.

Martin Heidegger says that to be human is to be always understanding, always feeling and always deciding. There is a vast philosophical discourse about his claims which I am dodging. I'm not trying to prove anything. I simply invite you to notice how everyday life gives you plenty of evidence supporting his claim. You are understanding and feeling – and deciding right now whether to put this book down or carry on reading.

This is the fundamental, existential situation in which we find ourselves – always understanding, always feeling and always deciding. It is a *process*. Our being is a process. Furthermore it is a demanding process – we must always decide how to be and how we respond to our feeling and understanding.

This is the challenge of our existence. It is not easy being human.

Enough already!

Let's go dancing.

Dance teachers analysed Lindy Hop and saw that there were many sequences of movement that took six beats or eight beats. So they taught 'six count' and 'eight count' moves. 'Six count' and 'eight count' are abstractions of just one part, albeit a basic part, of dancing. The originators of the dance never used those terms, but modern dancers often use them to describe moves, and beginners frequently think of the dance as made up of a sequence of 'six count' and 'eight count' moves.

When I first learned to dance I was obsessed with learning new moves and I performed as many as I could, enthusiastically, energetically and very badly. Like everyone else in the grip of a narrow, abstract understanding, I had no idea how much I did not know.

Focusing on the move is like going 'out' of reality to the simpler world of the abstraction. In order to dance properly, when we have learned from that abstraction we must come 'back' to the rich embodiment of the dance.

A couple who are doing moves are not yet dancing. They are still learning to dance. True dancing is a conversation with your partner, and sometimes with the musicians, to, and about, the music. The moves are like the words of a conversation. Sometimes you don't need a whole wor— Just as a good conversation is much more than 'saying words', so a good dance is much more than 'doing moves'.

Abstractions like 'eight count' help us to highlight elements and commonalities but we forget at our peril that they are always only a partial view.

Abstractions do not underlie reality; they are at best an insightful imposition on top of reality.

Abstractions are useful as a means to an end. We get into trouble when we mistake the means for the end.

About twelve years ago our research business was invited to pitch for some work by officials at the Department of the Environment. They wanted to know the extent to which 'sustainability thinking' was embedded in other UK government departments. At the briefing were two people from the Department of the Environment, one from the Sustainable Development Commission and a further representative from the Environment Agency. All of them were concerned with increasing 'sustainability thinking'.

On the one hand this represented admirable co-operation across different public-sector agencies. On the other it was a comical example of the enormous gap between abstract aspiration and practical reality. An obviously sustainable action would have been to cut the triplication of effort across three agencies, but such an idea was very far from the minds of our commissioners.

They were really asking us to find out if their policy of sustainability was being taken into account by other government departments making other policies.

This policy of researching policies sounds laudable on paper. Who would not want to increase sustainability, whether on ecological or economic grounds? Our experience suggests that in practice it would be an exercise in generating more reports and commissioning more research to inform creation of further protocols, committees and action plans. Real, immediate, practical action to decrease waste and increase sustainability was not on the agenda.

Abstractions such as 'sustainability thinking' are useful only in so far as they inform our practical actions. They are not a well-formed *goal* of action. We can go 'out' to think about notions of sustainability, but to act well we must come 'back' to embodied, contextual reality.

Our understanding goes astray when we imagine abstractions to be appropriate life goals. The challenge for all policies and abstractions is to see how they will translate into dynamic, observable life.

The only advert I ever ran as a hypnotherapist read,

Sort it out with hypnotherapy

followed by my phone number.

A person with a fear of flying could read it and understand that 'it' referred to their problem; a person who had panic attacks could understand that 'it' referred to *their* problem. Whatever the problem, that little phrase promised to solve it.

'It' is a non-specific reference. Hypnotists often use non-specific references. For example, to a subject in trance I might say, 'I'd like you to think back to the time when you first experienced the problems that you have come to see me about. And from this distant, safe place in the future now, I'd like you to imagine all the other possible events and understandings of that time and wonder how some of those can help you now.'

As you respond to this suggestion you remember a particular time, but I don't know any of the details. I have just elicited that memory by means of a string of non-specific references. 'Problem', 'events', 'understandings', 'that time', 'circumstances' – all of these are non-specific but can evoke specific items in the listening mind. Similarly I am inviting your mind to imagine how some of these insights can 'help you now' without specifying any content at all.

Drawing on cybernetic theory, analysts of hypnosis have proposed that a non-specific reference triggers a 'transderivational search', which causes the mind to search through memory to find items that fit the class it specifies. Here, for example, it will search for the time the subject first felt there was a problem.

I can use the same technique to craft therapeutic suggestions such as, 'I'd like you to imagine a time in the near future when all the things that worry you have been sorted out.'

A non-specific reference is essentially inclusive: if something *might* be included then it *will* be included. It also divides the contents of our awareness into two: that which fits within the reference and everything else.

But what is this 'transderivational search'? Is it not just another hypothetical abstraction? Have you ever seen one? Is it not just another abstract label passing itself off as an explanation?

Heidegger's insights offer us a deeper explanation. Remember Heidegger observes that we are always understanding ourselves and the world, and that of course includes all that we hear. When we hear a non-specific reference, we make sense of it. We understand it by finding referents.

This understanding or 'making sense' is not a special activity triggered by a non-specific reference. Heidegger points out that we are *always* making sense. In fact, making sense is *what we are.*

So we *cannot help* but make some sense of a non-specific reference. I can do so in many ways. I could notice, 'Oh look, there's a non-specific reference' but usually I won't. I will usually understand it by means of examples.

'Think of a time of delicious relaxation' is a non-specific reference. We make sense of it by recalling or imagining examples – playing in the park, sunbathing on a beach, hearing waves crashing on the sand, listening to beautiful music, lying in a luxury hotel bed, having a wonderful massage, and so on.

Neither Heidegger nor I claim that the sense we make of our world is accurate or complete. We just note that all the time we keep making some sense or other of our situation.

Non-specific references can easily be therapeutic. For example, now, dear reader, I would like you to think of a time when someone paid you a compliment. Maybe long ago, maybe yesterday. Take as much time as you need to go back to that time and remember it vividly – what you could see, what you heard, what you felt. Make the memory brighter and clearer and richer until you can really feel how it is to be complimented.

Be my guest.

You might notice that you had to focus a little bit to do that. You have to pay attention to your memory, and as you only have a limited amount of attention, you pay a little less attention to your surroundings. Hypnosis entails, among other things, the re-direction of attention. Non-specific references are hypnotic when they set up a feedback loop which pulls the attention deeper into the experience on which it is focused. For example:

'I'd like you to notice just how relaxing that relaxation can be and let your attention explore the details and feelings of the most rewarding part of your experience now.'

The power of the hypnotic engagement is enhanced if the focal concept is rewarding and there are compelling external reasons to seek the reward it offers.

A non-specific reference can generate several effects:

- It can provoke an automatic search through all of a person's memory and awareness.
- It can divide experience into two sets: that which fits within the reference and everything else.
- It can lead into hypnotic feedback loop.

You can't stop making sense of things. You just can't be sure it is the right sense.

8

HYPNOTIZING

The first time I deliberately hypnotized someone I didn't do it deliberately. I was still at university and I had learned a party trick during the vacation which involved pretending to hypnotize someone.

One evening with a gang of friends I asked, 'Who wants to be hypnotized?'

I had a volunteer. I handed him a plate to hold vertically in front of himself. I held one in the same position. My victim could not see that the back of his plate was covered in soot.

I told him to look into my eyes and ... well, I won't tell you exactly what I said.

I asked him to imitate what I was doing, and as I talked I ran my finger around the back of my plate and then ran it over my face.

The joke was meant to be that he would unwittingly paint his own face with the soot from the back of his plate.

But his hand didn't move at all. His face lost muscle tone and he just stared at me.

Dammit, I thought to myself. He knows this trick and he is pretending to be hypnotized so that he doesn't have to paint his face. 'Oh forget it,' I said out loud.

That was unfortunate.

As you know now, but I did not then, 'it' is a non-specific reference.

It was like I told him to format his hard disk.

He forgot everything.

Within a few moments he looked terrified.

I had no idea what was going on.

Luckily a friend saw his distress and called his name and gave him a hug and in a few more moments he awoke and was fine.

He told us that he had found himself in the void. Aware but with no idea of who he was, where he was, what was happening or anything around him at all.

It was no surprise he was distressed.

I apologized.

I felt embarrassed and very stupid indeed. A few years later I met a hypnotherapist at a party and asked her what I had done. Answering that question led me to train in hypnotherapy and thus I became a hypnotherapist.

There is a paradox at the heart of hypnotherapy. Many clients come to see you with a feeling or a behaviour or a habit they want you to take away. Please cure my depression, stop me smoking, change my diet and so on. They walk into the consulting room and say, in essence:

'Here's my life. Please fix it and give it back to me.'

I think of therapy as helping people to take charge of their life, to become more empowered rather than have more things done to or for them, so after a while I used hypnosis less frequently.

I also came to see that at least a good part of my work was not to hypnotize people but to *de*-hypnotize them.

Many clients were blanking reality – in hypnotic terms, had a negative hallucination – for events in their lives that were traumatic. Problems arose when they had the same automatic 'blanking' reaction to incidents in their present life which resembled their earlier trauma.

I had a client, for example, who had an abusive father and a series of abusive boyfriends. She would tell me of yet another incident of gaslighting or exploitation and then dismiss it with the phrase, 'That's fine', as though she was a strong woman who could just pick herself up and move on.

She did indeed pick herself up and move on. Then she would repeat the pattern with yet another man. In reality she was grievously and repeatedly hurt but her 'That's fine' was a trigger to hypnotically anaesthetize herself.

She needed to feel that hurt enough to learn what it meant for her and to learn how to avoid getting hurt like that again.

There is another paradox about hypnosis. There has been a great deal of research into hypnosis, but no one has managed to identify a measurement of brain activity corresponding to trance. There is no characteristic electroencephalogram (EEG) signature of hypnosis.

Many researchers therefore claim that hypnosis does not exist. Some say that people simply go along with hypnotic suggestions because they imagine that is what is expected. That is a reasonable conclusion but there is, logically, another reasonable conclusion which is that there is no discernible difference between the EEG signature of the ordinary waking state and that of hypnosis because they are the same state.

It follows that hypnotic phenomena are a part of everyday life. You can, for example, have a spontaneous analgesia if you stub your toe while running for a bus. You only feel the pain when you are safely seated on board the bus.

The notion that we are more hypnotized than we realize may explain why I found myself doing more de-hypnosis than hypnosis.

As an undergraduate studying Ancient History I received a small grant to go and look at archaeological sites in Italy. I went down to Herculaneum near Naples and then hitchhiked north again. I was wearing an old pair of rugby shorts which were very faded, very comfortable and very short.

Somewhere south of Rome a man stopped to pick me up. My Italian was very basic so we could hardly talk. After five minutes or so he put his hand on my knee.

My immediate thought was, 'You mustn't be prejudiced.'

Yep, that is exactly what I thought.

He tried to move his hand towards my groin. I pushed it back towards my knee. He pushed back. I pushed back. So it went for ten minutes, during which time I did not once try to take his hand off my knee.

Looking back now, how could we describe my state of mind?

Eventually I said, 'Here. Here! *Qui. Qui!*'

He stopped the car, I got out and he drove off.

To the left was a pebbly beach and the sea; to the right scrubland. I went into the sea and washed myself over and over and over again. I could not understand how his groping made me feel so dirty, but it did. I washed and washed. Then, very washed but still not feeling clean, I got out of the sea and went back up to the road.

There was absolutely nothing to be seen in either direction. Just empty road. So I stuck out my thumb. Eventually a man stopped. I got in the car.

He talked at me. It was clear that I didn't understand him, but he carried on talking. Non-stop.

After a while he started moving his hands. He didn't touch me but he touched the dashboard, the roof, the wheel, the door, the seat. It became a continuous, rhythmic, ritualistic tapping all around him.

He accelerated and started to use the horn.

As we came into the suburbs of Rome, the tapping and the driving became faster and faster and the horn more frequent.

Occasionally he seemed to ask me a question but he didn't stop talking. Then the horn was more or less continuous, the driving more terrifying and the tapping more and more furious.

'Here! Here! *Qui. Qui!*' I said.

He drove up on to the pavement and stopped. I grabbed my backpack and as I got out a police car zoomed up and two policemen jumped out, hands over their holsters.

I kept walking.

I later discovered that the trains in Italy were incredibly cheap. No one hitchhiked.

I have used hypnosis for decades.

I completed my PhD more than twenty five years ago.

I have induced countless trances.

But it was only in the last few years that the penny dropped.

The moment of illumination came when I realized that **abstractions are non-specific references.**

The degree of abstraction and the degree of non-specificity both vary enormously, but at least to some extent all abstractions are necessarily non-specific.

A non-specific reference can be hypnotic.

Abstractions can induce a trance.

Consider an abstraction like 'safety'. Safety is defined by its opposite: to be safe is to be protected from danger.

If I am seeking safety I consider my current situation and my future options and I seek out sources of danger in order to neutralize them.

This belief in safety can work like a non-specific reference. Everything either is or is not safe. Every possible danger becomes a danger that must be addressed. I could choose to accept a certain level of risk, but the more I 'believe in safety' the more I will insist on eliminating risk. The more risk I eliminate the more salient the remaining risks become and the more I will tend to wish to eliminate them too.

Trance behaviour begins when the abstraction gains priority over the perception of immediate reality.

Actions taken to increase safety generate a rewarding, albeit imprisoning, feedback loop. Eventually the belief in safety becomes a compelling focus of attention, which divorces awareness from everyday reality and proportion, and prevents the clear perception of reality and unintended consequences. It becomes a dysfunctional trance.

You might object that this is a far-fetched analysis of abstraction. Abstractions are an integral part of our language. If they really have the effect outlined above, it would imply that we are all in and out of some kind of hypnotic state for a great deal of our waking life!

And I would reply to your objection, 'Yes, it would, wouldn't it?'

The more you study hypnosis the more you realize that everyday consciousness is nothing like as conscious as we like to imagine.

An observable effect of trance is that many people believe what they are told uncritically. For example, at the beginning of his hypnosis show, Paul McKenna frequently suggested to his volunteers that they were riding race horses. A few people would leave the stage. Most would stay and act out riding a horse.

Recent events have demonstrated that vast numbers of people uncritically believe what they are told. Our language and the nature of our being render us perpetually at risk of mistaking abstraction for reality.

This hypnosis does not require a hypnotist, nor a malevolent conspiracy. It is built into the way we think. As Ludwig Wittgenstein, the greatest 20th-century philosopher in the Anglo-American tradition, wrote: 'Philosophy is a battle against the bewitchment of our intelligence by means of our language.'

Have another cup of tea.

Whenever a person takes an abstraction as self-evidently true or fundamental to reality, their perception and understanding are inescapably shaped by it. Their world view is distorted. I call such abstractions 'foundational abstractions'.

An ideology such as socialism or pacificism can be just such an abstraction. Ideologies are compellingly attractive because they solve a persistent existential problem. Humans cannot escape making meaning and making choices and we have no guarantee that our choices are good enough. Consequently anything that appears to let us know we are making the right choices is extremely appealing.

If you believe in an ideology it determines all your decision-making. It sets up an ongoing perusal of all your memories and behaviour and divides them into two sets: that which promotes or is congruent with the ideology, and everything else, which by default becomes 'against the ideology'.

This may seem far too simplistic to be plausible but, typically, ideologies in the first instance promote an attractive abstraction, such as 'safety' or 'liberation' or 'equality', so they develop a positive feedback loop. People feel good about pursuing 'safety' or 'liberation' or 'equality'.

Conformity to the ideology is rewarding and reinforcing so it begins to function hypnotically. Unfortunately the tenets of the ideology are necessarily fixed. As the world changes and people react to, or game, the ideology, its aims, however laudable in the beginning, become less and less fitting. At the same time, the ideologue on the inside of the trance becomes increasingly unable to see things from any other point of view. They feel right and every other opinion seems necessarily wrong. Over time they lose their sense of proportion and lose touch with everyday utilitarian understanding.

Ideologies combine the hypnotic function of abstraction with the three major disbenefits of literacy: abstraction, cognitive inertia and lack of emotional understanding.

Marx published his theories soon after the majority of the population of Europe achieved literacy, so his was the first 'great' ideology. The consequences became manifest everywhere Marxism was implemented. Stalin's Five-Year Plans, Mao Tse Tung's Great Leap Forward and the leadership of Pol Pot are all appalling examples.

I sometimes use the phrase 'cognitive capture' to refer to abstraction-induced trance. In this state we are unaware of the limitation of our thinking, in the same way that we do not see the edge of our own field of vision.

A specific contemporary example of cognitive capture is the application of patient choice and competition to the National Health Service in the UK. It seems unfair to keep picking on the NHS as there are many, many other examples, but I do so because it is such a clear illustration.

The NHS is far from efficient. In the abstract, competition encourages efficiency, lower prices, innovation and the development of desirable goods and services, so it would seem that competition would improve the NHS.

A policy of a competitive internal market was imposed on the NHS. It did not improve matters, because there was no understanding of the unique nature and context of the NHS.

The use of the NHS is almost always a distress purchase. Patients are driven by complex and urgent needs. They have little incentive to shop around, and they seek the absolute opposite of choice. They seek guidance and reassurance. It was breathtakingly stupid to consider patients in distress to be akin to savvy shoppers.

How did the policy-makers not see that?

How did Eddie not see his pipe?

So how do we escape these hypnotic traps? How did we end up here?

I was diverted by the temptation to explain how abstraction leads to hypnosis and that led me away from my intention to explore how things can go better. So easily do we lose ourselves, even into good intentions.

So every now and then we need to pause. To look around.

To ask ourselves, 'What's happening?'

'Was this my intention?'

Of course, many of you are very well organized. You would never get lost like this.

Anyway, let us pick up the thread.

At the end of chapter four we had a question that has not been completely answered: 'How do some people – some modern, literate people – understand more clearly?' But now we are better placed to address it.

There are many good answers to that question.

I will offer two here. First, a negative.

People who understand more clearly use abstractions but are not captured by them. In other words, they do not have foundational abstractions built into their world view.

Secondly, a positive.

Those people who see the world more clearly have benefited from a balanced education. Most have had a literacy-based education and all of them have been educated – formally or informally – by experience, apprenticeship and storytelling.

9
EMOTIONS

The taxis in Madagascar are almost all Citroën Deux Chevaux or Renault 4L. Ours was a 4L. When you hail a taxi, the first thing the driver will do is go to buy enough fuel to drive to your destination, which in our case was Morondava airport. We were intending to fly south to Toliara. Soon we had a puncture. We all got out of the car and the cause was clear. The centre of the tyre had been worn right down to the canvas. Our driver took out the spare and a spanner and started to undo the wheel nuts. A Renault 4L has three studs for each wheel. On this particular wheel two of the nuts were identical but the third was different and the spanner did not fit it.

We were on a rocky, sandy track a few miles out of town and some miles still from the airport. There were a few shacks, a few palm trees and a few people, but where could we possibly find the right size spanner?

My anxiety kicked in. 'We are going to miss our flight!'

A couple of minutes later a large, smiling man appeared with a hammer and a cold chisel. He crouched beside the wheel and with two blows, just two firm strikes, he reshaped the deviant nut. The spanner fitted perfectly. He went away, still smiling like Tom Bombadil, our driver changed the wheel, reusing the reshaped nut, and we made our flight with time to spare.

I was trapped in the idea of needing the correct spanner. Our saviour saw a more immediate remedy. He was also skilful. No measurement, no mark-up. Just two strikes. Freehand. I was unable even to think of the solution he delivered.

Later on that same trip we hired a driver with an ancient Peugeot 505. He drove out of a filling station straight across two lines of traffic, which was fairly bold even for Madagascar. It turned out that the steering had suddenly ceased to function.

It was a Sunday and we were at least 200 kilometres from our starting point.

By now I had learned a little. We found a patch of shade and sat down to read our books. Our driver crawled under the car, disassembled the steering system and pulled out the fractured central plate. About an hour and a half later a friend of a friend of his cousin turned up with the requisite spare part for the twenty-plus-year-old car. Our driver reassembled the steering and off we went.

In the 21st century we face many challenges. Some will say that the overwhelmingly important challenges are climate change, public health and social justice. Others will immediately yawn. Perhaps those issues raise serious questions. However, beneath all of them and many more social problems lie two personal challenges. We have touched on them both already.

The first is existential, the unfinished nature of our being. As Heidegger observed, we are beings who always have to decide how to be and we keep having to do it. We are always making meaning. How do we make a good enough meaning?

In modernity one of the easiest ways to deal with this existential challenge is to get a job. Somebody else tells you what to do and a thousand other decisions get made as a consequence. You have to live where you need to live for work, wear what you need to wear for work, and so on and so on. You also get paid.

Another popular choice, which can be combined with working, is to pick a group and do what everyone else in that group does. For example, if you are a Christian, the Church tells you what to do. Even if you fail to do it, the Church tells you to keep trying.

If you are a Muslim, you have a similar option. Do whatever your strand of Islam dictates. Every day, all your decisions are simplified.

Not surprisingly these options are very popular. They don't make the fundamental questions go away, but they provide firm guidance about how to answer them.

A similarly popular choice is to focus on accumulating money, which may or may not entail working for someone else. This choice is the foundation of modern consumerism and for a large group of people it is very rewarding indeed. I call them 'The People of the Graph' – they live between lines A and B.

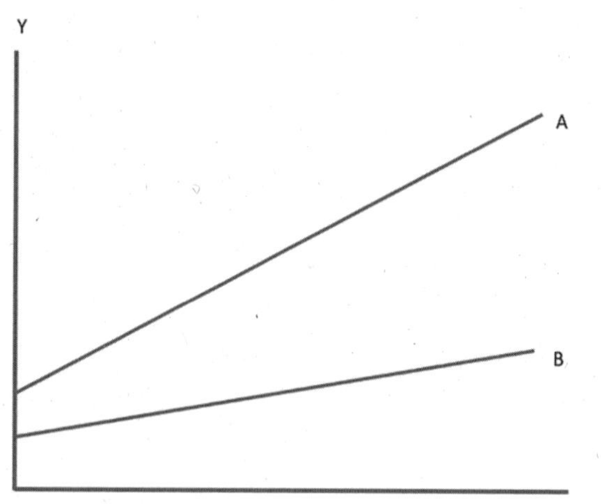

This is the graph. The x axis is time, the y axis is wealth. When you start working you have very little money. Maybe you have a bicycle. After a little while you can afford a small, old car. Time passes, you get a better job, more money and a better car. One day you get a new car, a Fiat, then a Ford, next a Toyota, a Mercedes. As time passes, so long as you stay between lines A and B, capitalism and consumerism work for you. Your entire life is evidence of its success.

People who fall below line B stop getting richer. Some flatline, some go broke. Capitalism isn't so great down there.

The people above line A have different problems. They have lots of money, but money doesn't give their lives any meaning. There is no sense of achievement cashing another cheque from your trust fund. Too many people up there get into trouble because they are overwhelmed by the possibilities of wealth and cannot find a satisfying way of life. Some fortunate innocents have a job and/or stay between lines A and B, or have a religious belief which answers their existential questions. But if religion, employment and wealth don't work for you, you will have to find your own solutions.

This brings us to the second fundamental challenge, which is cognitive. How do we handle our vulnerability to misunderstanding? How can we overcome the abstractions and inadequate assumptions built into mainstream thinking?

When times are hard, the flaws in conventional thinking become more evident. Doing what everyone else is doing leads to trouble. Luckily we have at least two sources of help:

> Many people have been this way before and they have left us helpful signposts. Literature has its upsides.
>
> Our own being is our own raw material. If we dare to be honest, we can use our own experience to improve our understanding and educate our emotions.

Emotions! We all have them, all the time, but they often trouble or confuse us. In recent times, there has been a movement towards more emotional honesty. So far, so good. If you feel bad, it is OK to say so. However, honesty is not enough. We need a deeper emotional education.

Emotions are not just random internal weather, nor a simple stop—go signal, nor an excuse for sentimentality. They can be an acute and sensitive form of perception. Outside formal education, much experiential learning is a matter of emotion. Questions about emotions come up all the time in therapy, so over time I came up with a few analogies.

Visualize a venetian blind, one of those window blinds with slim, horizontal slats. When it is closed, the faces of the slats are vertical and form a continuous surface. You can pull a cord and the slats rotate through 90 degrees to create openings in between.

Think of yourself as a venetian blind and an emotion as a wind. If you are closed when the wind blows against you, it pushes you about. If you are open, the wind will blow through you. The slats will flutter, then the wind will be gone.

In some ways emotions are like that. If you accept them and let them go through you, they pass, leaving a certain tremor behind. If you close yourself to them, if you reject them, they push and push and push you around. To put it another way, either you have your emotions, or your emotions have you.

This analogy may be helpful or may be misleading.

Here's another.

Imagine a membrane, like a very thin drumskin. It responds to every little anything that falls upon it from the outside. Our emotions can be sensitive like that – feeling an atmosphere, reacting to a person, responding to a situation.

This membrane also responds to things hitting it from the other side, from the inside. Our emotions are like that too – melancholy, joy, wariness, wonder and nameless other feelings arise within us.

Our emotions are our response to what is around us and what is inside us.

That analogy could be helpful or misleading too.

Here's a third one.

There is a children's party game called pass the parcel. Music plays as children pass a parcel around in a circle. When the music stops, the child holding the parcel takes off a layer of wrapping. The music starts again and, when it stops, another layer is taken off.

Our emotions are often like that parcel. Each time we stop, accept and hold an emotion, *the emotion unfolds to reveal something new …*

Imagine I read a certain news article and I feel angry. I pay attention to my anger and I can see what I am angry about. I realize I am angry because the article implies that people who disagree with government initiatives are stupid and dangerous. I realize I am frightened that people may believe the article is truthful. Beneath my anger lies fear. But why am I frightened? What is threatened? I search around to find what the fear is about. I fear losing the company of insightful friends and the freedom of a peaceable and rewarding life. If I pay attention to my anger like this it reveals something deeper. Beneath my fear lies care for the friends I treasure.

Here's a fourth analogy.

Emotions are like something else entirely. Add your own idea here. My ideas above are just similes, they don't capture what we can know about emotions. They just point towards an understanding.

As we educate our emotions – educate ourselves – we achieve emotional understanding. By emotional understanding I do not mean the concept popularized as 'emotional intelligence' in the book of that name by Daniel Goleman. Perhaps our analyses overlap but Goleman essentially puts emotional sensitivity in service of rationally determined ends. That is doubtless useful but that is not my interest.

I am interested in how emotional learning can reach further than rationality. It is subtle. It is exquisitely sensitive to context. It leads to insight and to seeing the world more clearly, but it cannot be subsumed to rationality. There is more to be learned, but there is only a very little I can usefully write here about emotional understanding. When we meet it, we know it is precious.

An unexpected consequence of emotional understanding is that the more you understand, the less there is to say. It is the opposite of building up a library of theories, explanations and data. Emotional understanding is more like removing barriers, expectations and delusions. The world is just as it is, and those who understand a little better see the world a little more clearly.

Perhaps your emotions are interactive puzzles. When you understand them they change you.

'I know I should go and visit my mum,' said Sally, 'but to be honest the thought of it does make me feel a bit .... well, I know I shouldn't, but, actually ...'

Her voice got a little quieter. 'I do feel a bit resentful. Do you know what I mean?'

There was a pause.

'Why should you visit your mum?' I asked.

'She's my mum!' said Sally. 'She's been having a hard time and, you know, she could do with some help. Family, you know.'

'The word "should" means that somewhere in your mind there is a rule,' I said, 'like "You should do this or that or whatever." What is the rule here?'

Sally thought for a moment. 'The rule is, "I should visit my mum."'

'When?' I asked. 'Every day? Every week? For how long?'

'Not every day!' She laughed. 'But ... every week or two?'

'OK, who wrote the rule?' I asked.

A slightly longer pause. 'Er ... my mum?'

I nodded. 'Probably. Anyway, Sally, do you still agree with it?'

Sally moved back a little and sat upright in her chair. 'No. I don't,' she said.

'Well,' I said, 'it's in your head, so why don't you write a new rule that you agree with?'

After my session with Sally, when I hear the word 'should' in my speech or anyone else's I often ask:

'What's the rule?'

'Who wrote it?'

'Do I still agree with it?'

My analogy about castles and windsurfers has many aspects that did not occur to me when it first came to mind. It is not just about security. It could also describe two different approaches to understanding.

We can build a collection of categories to organise our thinking and build them high enough to have a commanding view of the landscape around. Or we can go out to sea and fall in it again and again as we learn how to work with whatever comes our way.

Being a beginner at windsurfing is exhausting. Competent windsurfers use far less energy. They make it look easy, because it is easy for them. It doesn't require a lot of effort, just exactly the right effort.

Someone a long time ago remarked, 'Blessed are the ignorant and blessed are the wise. But woe to those on the path from ignorance to wisdom.'

It takes a lot of work to sort out the real from the unreal in our understanding. The situation is complicated by our tendency to become attached to our beliefs and emotions as much as to our possessions. The Buddha had a lot to say about attachment. I heard that somewhere he said, 'All suffering is caused by attachment to a previous state of existence.'

Zen Buddhism offers a description of itself in ten ox-herding pictures.

At the beginning a man is looking for his ox.

He finds his ox.

By the end he has no ox again, but the trees are in blossom.

10

TRUTH

A man was digging a hole. All of a sudden he threw down his spade.

'That's it!' he cried, 'I've had enough. I want to find the Truth.'

He left the hole, his job and his home and he set off.

Everywhere he went he asked people, 'Do you know the Truth? Where is the Truth?'

He travelled far and wide, hither and yon, uphill and down dale for years and years, always asking, always hunting.

Eventually he got a hint, which led to a clue, which led him to climb a far distant mountain. He climbed and he climbed until he reached a gully leading even further upwards. High in the gully wall he saw the entrance to a cave.

He clambered up to it and stepped in. He walked in, deeper and deeper into the mountainside, deeper and deeper into the darkness, but although it got very dark indeed he could still see just enough to put one foot in front of the other. He carried on and on until he began to see a little more. There was light, and yet more light. At last he came into a large cavern. He could see right across it, although he could not see where the light was coming from.

On the far side were two chairs and sitting on one of them was a very old, wrinkled, hunchbacked woman. She had greasy grey hair, a big black mole on her nose and a single, brown tooth.

'Come here,' she said, tapping the chair next to her. 'I've been expecting you.'

He walked across the cavern and sat down.

She looked at him, and as he looked back he was saturated by a wave of enlightenment. He could see the Truth.

He looked around in amazement. He understood.

Time slowed down.

Eventually he turned back to her.

'Thank you,' he said. 'You have answered the question I have been asking for years. Please tell me, is there anything I can do for you by way of thanks for this priceless gift?'

'Oh,' the old woman replied, 'when people ask about me, tell them I was beautiful.'

I have a long list of books I have not yet written. One of them is about choosing your career. The title is, *Find something you like doing, and get someone to pay you to do it.*

Like most self-help books the title is the best thing about it. In this case it is the only thing about it.

So:

'Find something you like doing, and get someone to pay you to do it.'

Simple to say, not so easy to do. The first half of that sentence could take years. How do we do it?

It is a classic example of how to learn from experience.

Start by taking the first opportunity you get. If someone offers you a job, accept it. Do it. Experience it. Learn whatever you can, and if you get bored start looking for the next opportunity. As soon as another opportunity comes up, take it. Do the next job. Repeat.

As soon as you get bored, start looking again. Each new job teaches you a bit more about what you don't like and a bit more what you do like. It doesn't matter which direction you set off in. Once you start moving, little by little you will be pointed in the direction of fulfilment. Sooner or later you will come across several opportunities at once and your experience to date will indicate which one is likely to be the most satisfying. Take it. You may be wrong, but if so you will learn something new. If you are right, you are moving closer to your goal. Keep going until you find you enjoy your job so much you don't want to move.

Is it really that simple?

No. There are lots of details to make that process easier. Keep your overheads low. Don't take on debt or a mortgage until you enjoy what you have to do to repay it. Do the job well; get a good reference.

The more curious and optimistic you are, the more opportunities you will meet.

You may come to a point where you know what you like doing and there are no jobs available doing that. So set up your own business. Employ yourself. If you enjoy your work you will work harder and better than those who are just doing it for the money.

Experience teaches us to pay attention at every level from the cash in our pockets to the feelings in our hearts.

That's all true, but it is just an abstract overview. You will only discover what, if anything, it means for you if you do it.

If it were possible to deliver in a book the benefits of experience, storytelling and apprenticeship we would not need experience, storytelling and apprenticeship.

Human beings are born unfinished. We need physical help until we can use our bodies, we need intellectual help until we can use our minds and we need emotional help until we can use our hearts. We don't always get what we need.

As mythologist Joseph Campbell put it: 'In order to aid personal development, mythology does not have to be reasonable, it doesn't have to be rational, it doesn't have to be true; it has to be comfortable, like a [marsupial] pouch. Your emotions grow in there until you're safe to get out. And with the dismemberment of the pouch – which is something that has happened in our world – you don't have that second womb. The rational attitude has said, "Oh these old myths, they're nonsense"; it has ripped the pouch to shreds. ... without this marsupial pouch, without this mythological pedagogy, the psyche comes out all twisted.'

In storytelling we gather up the scraps and patches of that torn pouch. We feel together – in both senses of that phrase. We feel gathered together with the teller and other listeners, and together we all feel the action of the story. And stories sneak past the categorical security guards ...

I was a teenager hanging out in a dark, smoke-filled room. I was sitting on the floor with some friends who had just constructed a bong with a rather terrifying capacity. There were two books on the carpet between us and someone was talking very enthusiastically about how amazing the book was.

'What?' I asked, pointing at a thriller. 'You mean this one?'

'No, no, no. That's bullshit. This,' he said, picking up a book by J. G. Bennett, 'this is *serious* bullshit.'

That was the first time I heard of Gurdjieff.

Heidegger doesn't write about 'human being'. He uses *Dasein*, meaning, in German, 'being there' – or more precisely 'there being'. If you read his work you begin to realize that he sees things differently. He doesn't start with an objective description of a human being; a conscious, rational mammal etc. He starts with 'what it is like to be a human being'.

For Heidegger, being is a *verb*. Humans happen. He says that we are always understanding, always feeling, always deciding. But he doesn't mean we are creatures who are always understanding, feeling and deciding. He means we *are* understanding, feeling, deciding. We are the process.

So, hang on, if I am this process, what is my body? Somewhere Heidegger remarks that the body is a very great problem for philosophy but he never gets round to addressing it. From his starting point it certainly is a problem. What exactly is the relationship between *Dasein* and the body?

There again, from the standard 'objective' point of view, we know a great deal about the body but consciousness remains a great mystery.

On the one hand, Heidegger's philosophy is difficult because it goes against what we take for granted. On the other hand, it is really simple. He just suggests that we notice what is really happening rather than go along with the ideas that have been handed down to us.

I mentioned earlier that Heidegger claims we are beings who always have to decide how to be. That may be true in principle but a perfectly reasonable objection, which you may already have raised, is: 'Well, *I* don't.'

I don't spend my time continually 'deciding how to be'. I have too much to do. I get up, I wash, I have breakfast, I go to work. If we are honest we cannot say we are constantly choosing a specific, definite way of acting or existing. We are just, to use a telling colloquialism, getting on with things.

According to Heidegger, the very casual, ordinary unthinkingness of this way of being has led philosophers to overlook its importance. This is how he puts it:

> Because this average everydayness makes up what is ontically proximal for this entity, it has again and again been passed over in explicating *Dasein*. That which is ontically closest and well known, is ontologically the farthest and not known at all; and its ontological signification is constantly overlooked.

I got a headache, remember? By the way, 'ontological' means 'pertaining to the philosophy of being' and 'ontically' — no! I can feel the dark tentacles reaching out from the philosophical forest. If you want to get into it, the internet beckons ...

Once again we are going to scoot around the forest and go straight to the output on the other side. Heidegger points out that we *can* make our very own decisions, based on our own unique situation and possibilities. However, most of the time we don't. We just do what people normally do.

This is the observation by means of which Heidegger approaches his notion of 'being-with' I mentioned earlier.

What people normally do is our being in common. What we have in common is ontologically *prior* to our unique possibilities.

What on earth does that mean?

Heidegger proposes that the way of being we have in common is the condition for the possibility of being unique. Put more crudely and inaccurately, we are not a number of individuals who come together to form a society. We are a collective which gives rise to the possibilities of some of us being individual.

A small, practical corollary of that slightly mind-boggling claim is this: every single word I am using here is inherited from writers before me. The possibility of writing something novel and unique arises from the common language that we already share.

They were so foolish in the past, weren't they? Before Progress.

Witch hunts! Dancing mania! Tulips! Ha! Thank goodness we know better now.

One evening I was cycling up Highgate West Hill – quite a steep hill, quite a long hill – and wishing fervently that when I got to my destination there would be no one there. I was exhausted, not just physically but emotionally.

I had established a little storytelling club at the Raj tea rooms at the top of the hill and this evening it was my turn to tell. The Raj was run by Darcy Brewster, a wonderful, welcoming bear of a man with a twinkle in his eye and a taste for the off-beat and vintage. He was happy for me to tell stories because my audience would buy his food and drink.

But that evening I didn't want an audience at all. I wanted to get there, show my face to show willing and go home to bed. I locked up my bike, made my way through the dress shop (the only way into the tea rooms was through a dress shop) and climbed up the dark, wooden stairs. The Raj was a very small venue and it was packed. There was not a single spare seat. There were people sitting on tables. I couldn't go home.

When I stood up before my audience, energy arrived. My stories opened like blossoming roses. The show that evening was delightful.

All performers know this – coming on stage and feeling the energy you receive from your audience. We all know it. We can feel it. But what *exactly* is it? What is going on that we feel so vividly and yet cannot define or quantify? If it is a physiological response of arousal, and surely it is at least that, why can't I turn it on myself? Certainly I can recall it, I can imagine it vividly and feel it echo – but the real thing, that's a bit more.

Now, many years later, I have an inkling of an answer to that question.

Heideggerian ontology implies that human beings are always already being together. We always feel each other. But there is so much suffering and vulnerability and inner chaos that it is enormously demanding to be fully conscious of each other. So we have learned to be tactful and defend ourselves. We politely ignore what we feel. Every day trains are full of commuters pretending not to notice what they have just noticed about each other.

When a story is well told we feel the story, and as we do so we all feel together, and a great energy is released as we reconnect to each other.

Understanding is not the agglomeration of knowledge, just as a pile of bricks is not a house. Bricks must be assembled in a certain way to make a house. Understanding is not even a neat, house-shaped pile of knowledge. Understanding is not a possession or a quality or a database.

Understanding is an event.

When we understand we perceive our environment and acknowledge our analysis and projection. We see how things are disposed in this moment – how it has arisen and the many ways it may go. The more we understand, the more clearly we see, the sharper the focus, the finer the colour, the greater the depth of field and the wider, deeper and larger the context in both space and time.

True understanding is true in-sight. Today, for some little time, I understand a little. Later, when I am tired, when I have a headache or a beer, I understand less. Understanding happens and then it passes. It must happen many times before the memory is sufficient for us to see more clearly more of the time.

We all know this. You can tell, by observing yourself right now, that for all but the most trivial of insights we have to concentrate or focus in some way. Yet we all casually talk about our understanding as though it is a sort of quality or possession. We like to flatter ourselves.

In a TV interview in 1952, aristocrat and philosopher Bertrand Russell said:

> One of the troubles of the world has been the habit of dogmatically believing something or other and I think all these matters are full of doubt and the rational man will not be too sure that he is right. ... We ought always to entertain our opinions with some measure of doubt.

Please stay with me for one more bit of strangeness. For the moment, let's concede that we *are* the process of understanding, feeling and deciding.

We are also, very obviously, yet in a way mysteriously, bodies.

What else are we?

We are our attention.

Right now you can choose to continue to pay attention to this text, or you could be distracted:

'I could do with a coffee.'

'It's time to walk the dog.'

'Has somebody liked my post?'

We like to imagine that we are in charge of our attention, but much of the time it is not under control. It wanders off and gets caught. Buddhists call this 'the monkey mind'. The possibility of getting distracted and caught is massively enhanced by media algorithms. We have electrified the monkey mind.

If our control of our attention is that weak, how do we concentrate long enough to get anything done? Much of the time we are driven by necessity, fear or greed. We go to work because we need food and shelter. We *fear* losing what we have. Necessity sends us out to work.

Some people don't work; they live off the charity of the state or others. Weirdly that doesn't make them particularly happy, but we don't have the space to go into that here. It is an interesting phenomenon but it is a *distraction*.

We are also motivated by *greed*. I want to turn left on boarding, I want fancy food, a fabulous holiday, a smart car, a bigger house and so on.

We can be motivated and focused by *worthwhile* activities. We feel pleased to do a good job well, to mend something broken, to make something beautiful, to help each other or to become more healthy.

A considerable appeal of conceptual thinking is that it corrals our attention. It gives reassuring boundaries to our understanding. A definition or a concept is like a finite geometric shape in an infinitely fractal world.

Abraham Maslow summed up the drivers of our behaviour with his famous hierarchy of needs, which is usually illustrated with a pyramid. At the bottom are food and shelter, at the top is self-actualization.

It's a neat diagram. But odd. Why is self-actualization a tiny little triangle at the top?

Why isn't it the other way round? Why not simple and narrow at the bottom and wide and wonderful at the top? Or why not like a tree, the trunk of food and shelter at the bottom and up at the very tips of the twigs and leaves the rich complexity of self-actualization?

We can direct our attention or let it be caught. We can retrieve it or drift away. We can witness ourselves or disappear into our own experience. We can forget what we were doing and get lost in our thinking. We can lose awareness of our bodies. We can find old habits triggered by chance associations. Hypnotists have words for these phenomena: trance, amnesia, analgesia, future-projection in time, positive and negative hallucinations, age regression, post-hypnotic suggestions. This is the stuff of everyday life.

Heidegger said that in everyday life *Dasein* is mostly *benommen* – 'dazed'. William Blake wrote of 'mind forg'd manacles'. Gurdjieff, who like Freud and Jung had a lot of experience with hypnosis, said man is in a hypnotic sleep.

G.I. Gurdjieff was a remarkable man. He offered an unconventional yet compelling interpretation of the human situation. He was in Russia at the time of the Revolution and made his way to Istanbul. He established his *Institute for the Harmonious Development of Man* in Fontainebleau, France, in 1923. The path to harmony was not a smooth one. Gurdjieff put considerable effort into making life difficult for the people around him. He aroused both fierce loyalty and strong condemnation.

Hannah Arendt reported that when Heidegger was in Marburg he was known as the 'hidden king of philosophy'. His reputation was based not on publication but on his lectures. In 1927 he became a professor in Marburg and published *Sein und Zeit* (*Being and Time*). The following year he was appointed professor of philosophy in Freiburg.

These were two very different, very peculiar, men; contemporaries in entirely disparate realms, yet there are curious elements of similarity.

Both wrote books that are extremely difficult to read. In *Being and Time* Heidegger was struggling to express his thoughts in a language already corrupted by the problems he was trying to reveal. He had to create new words in order to avoid the misunderstanding baked into everyday language. In *Beelzebub's Tales to his Grandson,* Gurdjieff was deliberately obtuse. He made up words as puzzles that hinted at what he meant but hid it as well. He wanted to force people to make an effort to understand.

Both thought that mainstream western thinking was founded in delusions and that we misunderstand our own being.

Heidegger wrote in *Being and Time* that his task was 'one in which ... we are to destroy the traditional content of ancient ontology until we arrive at those primordial experiences in which we achieved our first ways of determining the nature of Being.'

Gurdjieff described the mission of *Beelzebub's Tales to his Grandson* as: 'to destroy, mercilessly, without any compromises whatsoever, in the mentation and feelings of the reader, the beliefs and views, by centuries rooted in him, about everything existing in the world.'

Both thought that most of us most of the time do not rise to our unique potential but follow the herd, doing what 'one does'.

Both wrote that conscience has a special role in our being.

The philosophy of Martin Heidegger is deep, original and profound and has been central to the academic canon for nearly one hundred years.

Gurdjieff was widely considered to be some kind of weirdo, a cultish conman with ridiculous theories about food for the moon, rays of creation and ancient wisdom.

How can I possibly refer to these two men on the same page? It is an offence against the widely accepted categories of Western thought! Oops. Categories again.

Now we are a few steps beyond bite-sized philosophy and storytelling. Is it getting absurd or too serious? It's up to you. This isn't a proper argument. I'm not even trying to persuade you. It's more an invitation to a point of view. You can skim past this stuff if it is not your thing.

Where Heidegger was a thinker, Gurdjieff was a practical man. He proposed that in order to sort ourselves out we must observe ourselves as honestly as possible. That takes effort. It is hard even to remember to do it. As he put it: 'We forget ourselves.'

With persistence, assistance and good fortune, little by little we may observe what is happening within us, but that is just the beginning of our troubles. We love to run ahead of ourselves to the security of pseudo-understanding. We jump to a pre-existent concept and say, 'Ah yes, I see! This is me now.'

Gurdjieff called this 'wiseacreing'. Heidegger called it 'idle talk'.

This happens over and over again. It happens *automatically*, but if we make an effort to bring consciousness, to retrieve our attention, something else may happen. As we observe the chaotic torrent of our awareness we may see that amid our feelings are messages from our deeper selves, our conscience. They are nearly always mangled and mistranslated and misunderstood so we have to work with great patience and care to discern, unfold and understand them.

We need to unfold our emotions repeatedly in order to begin to understand them – that is to say to understand ourselves – clearly. And that is just the beginning of understanding just one part of ourselves.

A balanced education never ends. We are so easily hypnotized by charming concepts. We must grasp these concepts, but not be grasped by them. Our task is to repeatedly de-hypnotize ourselves, to master our attention and rise to the challenge of the understanding, feeling and deciding, which is our being.

Ah, such a noble task! How uplifting! How enchanting! Already I can feel a spiritual awakening! Come! Come!

Or is this just new age nonsense? What is a 'deeper self'? Given repeated proof of mankind's capacity for barbarity, is 'conscience' anything other than wishful thinking?

For a long time I lived in Kings Cross, towards the north of central London. I had friends in Chelsea in the south-west of central London.

One evening I was cycling to their house for dinner. I came along Oxford Street and into Hyde Park. It is always delightful cycling into the park. It is like passing through an invisible wall into the fresh, cooler, softer air. It was a beautiful, dusky evening. I went south through the park heading for the exit next to the hideous new billionaire apartment block built by the Candy brothers.

As I approached the edge of the park a heron flew past me, close and low. It was instantly uplifting – a delightful moment of closeness to nature. As I was savouring that moment, two more herons came past. Extraordinary!

Then I saw that to the right of the path ahead was a little lawn surrounded by low, black metal railings. Gathered there were a dozen or more herons. Two walkers had stopped to look at them. I also stopped and stood astride my bike, gazing.

As we all stood there – walkers, herons and me – a little old lady came across the road from the billionaires' building. She obviously wasn't a billionaire. She was pushing one of those old, upright, rectangular shopping bags on wheels, half bag, half walking frame.

She came up to the railings, opened the top of her bag and pulled out some bread. She held out little pieces and the herons came to her.

As she fed them she greeted each one, 'James. James. James ...'

I watched for a while, then quietly moved on.

As I cycled along Pont Street I realized what was happening. She was obviously a widow. Her husband had died and had been reincarnated as a heron, but she could not tell which heron he was, so she was feeding them all.

The whole episode, the twilight, the herons, her devotion and generosity, suffused me with an extraordinary joy.

It was not until I was chaining up my bike outside my destination that I understood my realization was absurdly romantic. There is a far simpler explanation.

Probably all herons are called James.

11

A YAKUT STORY

Round about the year 2000 I went to New York to attend a weekend workshop on playback, process work and social action. Playback is the improvised theatre mentioned earlier, process work is a form of group psychotherapy created by Arnold Mindell, a post-Jungian bodyworker, and social action – well, I didn't really know at the time. Maybe I should have done my research.

The workshop was held at a retreat centre in the countryside an hour or two's drive from New York City. The leaders were a slow-moving, dignified black man and a slim, talkative white woman. I have forgotten both their names, but I remember that he introduced himself as having ancestry from Ghana. The first morning there was a lot of process work and discussion of social action but no playback. A little while into the afternoon I asked, 'Can we do some playback now?'

A voice rang out, 'That's racist.'

I was completely surprised.

'No,' I said. 'I would just like to do some playback.'

'You are a white man challenging the leader of this workshop who is black. You are being racist.'

'No, really,' I replied. 'I'm just making a request.'

Process work amplifies the unspoken feelings and dynamics of a person or a group in order to develop and resolve them. Members of the group align themselves as they feel moved with whatever positions come up and respond from there to what happens next.

The theory is that whatever we are conscious of at a certain time is our primary process. However, beneath that is another process labelled the secondary process. If we overcome our resistance to change the secondary process emerges and becomes the primary process. Beneath that there will be another secondary process and so on. It is a fascinating and often volatile approach to personal and group dynamics. Like unwrapping the parcel of individual emotions, it can deliver unexpected insights.

A piece of process work kicked off. I was bewildered. It was clear that there was a lot of emotion in the room, but it didn't belong to me. At one point a tall, thin, white man told me in a condescending tone, 'I can hear the condescension in your voice.'

Others insisted I was racist even if I was not aware of it. My own experience was completely the opposite. I had been positively impressed by our workshop leader and was more interested in his presence than his race. I hoped to get to know him better.

Eventually the process fizzled out. Thereafter there was a peculiar atmosphere because they were clearly expecting some kind of gesture of repentance, but search though I did, I found nothing to repent. The following afternoon at the final session I was invited to speak. I told a story.

Seven brothers were playing their favourite game. They stuck little sticks into the ground and threw stones to knock them down.

A squirrel came out of the forest and said, 'I want to play. Let me play!'

'You can't play,' said the brothers, 'you're a squirrel.'

'I want to, I want to, I want to!' said the squirrel.

He wouldn't shut up so the brothers let him play. He had a go. He was no good.

The next turn, one of the brothers threw a stone that bounced off a stick and hit the squirrel.

'You hit me, you hit me!' screamed the squirrel. 'I'm going to get all my brothers and cousins and uncles and we are going to beat you up!' and he ran off back into the forest.

The brothers were naturally terrified. Where could they hide?

They thought about running away but they knew the squirrels would catch them.

'What can we do? What can we do?'

'I know,' said the youngest brother. 'We can hide in the sky!'

They all realized this was a brilliant idea and were just about to go when the youngest brother spoke again, 'What about our sister?'

She couldn't hide in the sky, so where could she hide?

The oldest brother had another brilliant idea and suggested that she hide underground.

So they went into their yurt and dug a hole in the ground and the sister lay down in it and they put a little bag of fox blood on her chest and gave her a reed to breathe through, then they covered her over and stamped down the earth and went outside again.

The oldest brother fired an arrow up into the air, so hard and so high that it stuck into the top of the sky. The second brother fired an arrow so hard and so high that it stuck into the first brother's arrow. The third brother fired an arrow so hard and so high that it stuck into the second brother's arrow. The fourth brother ... and so on and so on until the seventh brother fired an arrow that stuck into the sixth brother's arrow and it was just low enough that they could jump up and catch it and one by one they climbed up into the sky. As the seventh brother climbed up he pulled up the arrows behind him and just as he reached the very top an army of furious squirrels came out of the woods, armed to the teeth and looking for vengeance.

They became even more angry when they couldn't find the brothers. They ransacked the yurt and interrogated everything inside.

'Where are they hiding? Where are they hiding?'

The pots and blankets and chest and rugs stayed silent, but a frightened pair of felt boots cracked.

'There's someone hiding under the yurt,' they admitted.

'Ha!' the squirrels shouted and they began to stab the ground with their spears and knives and daggers.

The chief squirrel held up his spear. The tip was covered in blood.

The squirrels screamed and shouted in triumph and ran back into the forest.

The little bag of fox blood had done its job. The girl waited until it had been quiet a long time and then dug her way out.

Everything in the yurt was smashed and broken. She went outside. She was alone. She set off to look for her brothers.

She walked and she walked and she walked. She walked into the forest and she carried on walking. She met a frog.

'Hellooooo,' croaked the frog. 'That's a pretty dress you are wearing.'

'Thank you,' said the girl.

'Would you like some tea?' asked the frog.

'Yes, please,' said the girl.

'Follow me,' said the frog and she led the girl to her yurt.

The frog lifted the flap and went in first. As the girl ducked and stepped inside the frog bashed her on the head with a log and knocked her out.

She woke up to the sound of horses' hooves approaching. Her dress had gone. She peeked outside and saw the frog preening herself in her dress and two young men approaching on horseback.

The young men dismounted.

'What a beautiful dress!' said the older brother.

'Oh thank you,' simpered the frog.

The younger brother felt left out. He walked towards the yurt.

The girl was terrified. She was naked. Just as the younger brother lifted the flap of the yurt she hid herself inside a wooden stick.

The younger brother picked up the stick and started carving it.

Outside things were going well.

'Will you marry me?' asked the older brother.

'Oh yes!' sighed the frog, so he picked her up, put her in front of him on the saddle and rode off to tell his father.

Inside the yurt the younger brother was whittling away at the stick when a drop of blood appeared.

He dropped the stick in shock. It split in half and out stepped a beautiful, naked woman.

His jaw dropped, his eyes popped and his heart leapt.

'Wait!' he said.

He ran to his horse, grabbed a blanket and gave it to her to wrap around herself.

'Will you marry me?' he asked.

'Oh yes,' she said and her eyes filled with tears of joy.

The younger brother picked her up, put her on his horse, and they rode off to tell his father.

Meanwhile, the older brother was introducing his bride-to-be to his father.

'Now, my dear,' said his father, 'tell me about your family. Who are your people?'

'That's easy,' said the frog. 'Can I borrow a bucket?'

She went to the river and came back with a bucket of water.

'Look,' she said.

Everybody looked into the bucket and there in the water, swimming round and round and round, were a family of frogs.

Suddenly the brother and the father and everyone else realized that the bride standing in front of them was a frog!

'You can't marry my son,' said the father. 'Get out of here!' and they ripped the dress off her back and the frog hopped away as fast as she could.

At that moment the younger brother rode up and he said, 'Father, Father, I have found myself a bride.'

The father looked at the young woman wrapped in a blanket and he said, 'Now, my dear, tell me about your family. Who are your people?'

'I have seven brothers,' said the girl, 'but I don't know where they are. I was looking for them when I met your son.'

'I won't be fooled again,' said the father. 'You cannot marry my son unless I can meet your family.'

He sent her away.

She walked out alone into the darkening forest. She had nowhere to go. She just walked, crying and calling for her brothers.

The Enduri, the spirits of the sky, heard her crying and calling.

They went to her brothers and said, 'Your sister is down on the earth and she is crying and calling for you.'

The brothers came tumbling down out of the sky and said, 'Sister, sister, we are so sorry. Up in the sky we forgot about you.'

She told them that she wanted to get married and she needed her family.

The brothers went back up into the sky and came down again with a wedding dress woven from moonlight and stardust and they all went back to the family of her betrothed.

The young man's father greeted the seven brothers warmly and agreed to let his son marry their sister.

The wedding feast lasted for three days and three nights.

After the feast the brothers said, 'Sister, we live in the sky now. We will always look out for you. If you need us, call and we will come down.'

Their sister and her husband lived a good life and had many children. The brothers returned to the sky. You can still see them every night.

That story is from the Yakut people of Northern Siberia. It is one of my favourite stories, but I have no idea why it sprang to mind on that day. On the way back to New York City the minivan took a different route. We came over a bridge on to the northern end of Manhattan Island and drove through Harlem. For twenty or thirty blocks I did not see a single white face. I had never seen segregation like that anywhere in Europe. I became a little less puzzled by the behaviour of my fellow workshop participants.

Abstraction, cognitive inertia and lack of emotional understanding are all around us. They are such ordinary habits of thought that we don't notice how much they direct our thinking. They feel so natural we rarely notice that we could think differently. Unfortunately they often generate bad answers to good questions.

It is commonplace to assume that we must have good policies and protocols for every eventuality. Whatever the problem, we need a protocol, a policy or a law, to fix it. But there is an alternative.

As Native American leader Oren Lyons, the literate heir of a non-literate tradition, explained to Jerry Mander in *The Absence of the Sacred*: 'We really don't have the kind of specific rules or laws that you have. Nothing is ever written down. ... If you write the rules down, then you have to deal with the rule rather than figuring out what's fair. We're interested in principle. The principle is to be fair. ... We have all the problems any community has. When one member intrudes on another, we have a situation. We meet and just keep talking until there is nothing left but the obvious truth, and both families agree on the solution.'

'Huh', I thought when I first read that, 'that's all very well if you have all the time in the world. What about people with jobs and responsibilities and so on? They can't sit around talking for ever.'

In spite of my initial pushback, I kept wondering about his words. Oren Lyons didn't say they talked for ever, just until they agreed on a solution. Nor did he say they had to talk continuously. The more I wondered, the more it made sense. And is the alternative really such a great idea? What about the rules and policies and legislation that cause problems for millions of people?

To take a hideous example, talking would surely have been better than the decades of injustice and suffering created by the UK Post Office's refusal to discuss the dysfunctionality of its Horizon accounting system. British sub-postmasters were persecuted because of software failings over which they had no control. The Post Office bankrupted honest people and drove some to suicide.

At the time of writing, Paula Vennels, former chief executive of the Post Office, is still an Anglican priest, albeit without a parish. It is difficult to tell which is more derelict, the church or its minister.

The closer people are to practical tasks and to direct, personally felt feedback from their actions, the more likely they are to make sound decisions. The more heavily people are involved in abstract analysis and policy-making, the more likely they are to make bad decisions.

The absolute nadir of abstraction is an ideology which attempts to make an abstract notion real in the physical world. Even ideals such as equality, diversity and anti-racism will inevitably be perverted by the inherent distortions of ideology.

All ideologies are inadequate because:

- They are fixed in the language of their creation, hence limited by the vision of their creators and outdated as the world changes.
- They never achieve their designated goals because people fail to agree about what real situation corresponds to the abstract goal of the ideology.
- They tend to induce hypnotic tunnel vision.
- Their impersonal formulations lack recognition of the significance of personal, emotional relationships and emotionally or morally sophisticated understanding.
- They divert discussion away from reality and towards abstraction.
- The focus on abstract ideals causes people to ignore or belittle real situations and lived experience.
- People inevitably game ideologies in the pursuit of power and personal gain.

Jung saw this coming. In 1954 he wrote, 'Our blight is ideologies — they are the long-expected Antichrist!'

It doesn't have to be like that. If each of us does the right thing, vast social problems disappear. For example, there is a simple solution to racism. Follow these two principles:

Be fair.
Be polite.

We have evidence that this works. Millions of people of all races and colours *already* adhere to these two principles. In their lives, whether they be Hispanic or Asian or Black or White or whatever, where people strive to be fair and polite there is no racism.

Fairness and politeness generate direct and immediate benefits. Some people may need a lot of support to practise them. Some will fail or reject them and cause problems. It is not always easy to get it right, but it is always worth trying.

Principles are preferable to policies. Principles are like points of the compass. They guide your journey; they are not destinations.

When Paul McKenna launched his career as a hypnotist I worked with him to ensure that his stage show was completely safe. At one show we witnessed a striking event. Paul had a routine in which he would explain to his hypnotized subjects that he was holding a pair of magic spectacles: to men they would reveal the women in the audience naked; to women they would reveal the men in the audience naked. He would pass the spectacles along the line provoking enthusiastic responses.

He asked one woman if she saw anyone she fancied.

'Oh yes!' she said.

'Who is it?' Paul asked.

'Him,' she said, pointing. 'The one in the white shirt.'

She could see him naked and also point him out as wearing a white shirt. It was a perfect example of a hypnotic phenomenon first identified by researcher Martin Orne in 1959. He named it 'trance logic' wherein hypnotized subjects can simultaneously hold contradictory beliefs and ignore the contradiction.

Ernest Hilgard, another prolific researcher of hypnosis, discovered another version of the same phenomenon of dual consciousness. He hypnotized a subject and induced hypnotic anaesthesia. He then induced pain by immersing the subject's hand in ice-cold water. Even though the subject reported a total hypnotic anaesthesia, Hilgard was able to contact a part of the subject who could report the pain accurately.

Nowadays vast numbers of people in many differing fields have locked themselves into a negative hallucination to avoid the shame of being avidly, repeatedly and catastrophically wrong.

They manoeuvre to avoid open, honest discussion about dissenting points of view because at the deeper level of Hilgard's 'hidden observer' they know. Trance logic allows them also to refuse to admit that they are refusing to engage their critical faculties.

The internet has made possible the global dissemination of these delusions.

Never have so many been so wrong about so much.

12

A BABEL STORY

Here's a Hollywood joke:

> 'Money isn't everything.'
> 'You're not rich, are you?'

I very much enjoy qualitative research. It is not uncommon at the end of a one-hour in-depth interview for the interviewee to remark, 'I enjoyed that. I hardly ever have the time to stop and think about my job. It was very interesting.'

Most therapy is also a one-hour one-to-one conversation. People reflect on their own situation, tell stories and after a while they see themselves, their own story, differently. I have indicated how storytelling can bring about existential transformation, but I'm trying to keep the philosophy under control in this book. Perhaps we can go into more detail another time.

The lesser point I wish to make here is that in my experience people very much enjoy thinking but don't do it as much as they would like. They are too busy or they are discouraged by education, by experts, by self-help books or the television or the internet.

Thinking deeply is rather like cooking. It is enjoyable and nourishing but if you get out of the habit you can live without it. You could get your opinions from Pizza Hut.

In the 1990s I attended the private view of a friend's paintings. Another artist in the same exhibition, Minna Thornton, had some beautifully drawn desert pictures and an intriguing impressionist portrait of her father.

I suggested to my siblings that we commission a portrait of our father. They chipped in, and Minna came to my parents' house to paint. They had several sessions, which my father enjoyed.

I received a phone call from my father.

'Minna would like you to go and see the portrait,' he said. 'I think the mouth needs fixing.'

I was busily doing business around town but I quickly dropped into Minna's studio to view the portrait.

I could see what my father meant about the mouth. It was a sort of slash of paint, but as I looked suddenly, for a moment, I saw my father looking at me. I recognized exactly his look of interested enquiry. I carried on examining the picture, and then another flash – his way of looking slightly downwards, thoughtful and pondering. I was lost for a few moments seeing one expression after another.

I remembered my father's concern and my duty to report it.

'It's great,' I said. 'My father thinks the mouth needs fixing.'

'OK,' said Minna.

A couple of weeks later the portrait was delivered. The mouth was fixed. It was a good likeness, an excellent portrait.

All the wondrous moments of expression had gone.

I dutifully assumed, without thinking, that my task was to deliver my father's wishes for a little tidying up. I saw the magic that Minna had created, but I did not tell her. I assumed she could keep my father happy and keep the magical mosaic. I did not check. I did my duty but I did not speak up for the genius that I had seen.

My father died in 2006.

My thoughtless assumptions hurt to this day.

There are many elephants in the room. My original intention was to catch them, illuminate them vividly and interrogate them. I wanted to make them unforgettably visible to everyone. I had it planned somewhere around chapter seven.

But I've changed my mind.

There's no point.

Everyone knows about the elephants. Even those people who are struggling desperately to not see them are very careful to avoid them. They don't want to come out of trance, hence the fervour of their attacks on anyone who disagrees with them about the Complete Absence of Elephants.

Of course, many of the people who do know about the elephants disagree with each other. Like the famous blind men walking through the jungle who encounter an elephant, each one of them knows what he has *really* found.

The one holding on to a leg knows he has found a tree.

The one holding the trunk has found a snake.

The one holding the ear realizes it is a fan.

The one touching the flank believes it is a wall, and so on.

There are elephants and there are woozles. Winnie the Pooh and his friend Piglet go hunting for woozles. They find their tracks and follow them. As they do so they see more and more woozles are joining the group. Eventually they realized they are following their own tracks round and round in circles.

A woozle is a very low-quality academic paper which nevertheless gains credibility and high status because it is repeatedly cited, and papers which cite it are cited, and so on and on.

The world's most famous woozle is an academic paper by John Cook *et al* claiming that 97 per cent of the world's scientists believe in dangerous man-made global warming. It is endlessly cited, although many reviews have pointed out its flaws. Most recently David Craig re-examined it. (His analysis, and the original paper, are worth reading; see the notes at the end.) Craig shows that multiple chicaneries were used to generate the figure of 97 per cent. The data used in the paper itself reveal that only 8.2 per cent of the abstracts reviewed explicitly agreed with the theory of man-made global warming. On reflection it is most peculiar that John Cook's woozle is cited at all because consensus is irrelevant to the progress of science. Indeed many, following Popper, would say science proceeds by overturning the consensus.

So many woozles!
So many elephants!
Our room is crowded.

I was asked by a friend of a friend to crew his yacht, which he was moving from somewhere on the east coast down to Falmouth in Cornwall. I was to do the leg from Weymouth to Dartmouth. I hadn't sailed for a long time so I was happy to take the opportunity.

I met him early in the morning and we set off straight away. He was skipper and navigator so I just expected to do as I was told.

We sailed south-east to clear Portland Bill and then turned west across the bay towards Dartmouth. The wind was not very strong, perhaps force 2, and quite fine on the port bow. We weren't making enough way under sail, so the skipper started the engine and we kept the mainsail up close-hauled for a bit of assistance.

It was a lovely, sunny day. I was on the helm and enjoying myself. The sea started to get a bit strange. Normally in open water waves mostly come from one direction. When the wind changes it can get messy but generally there is a sort of rhythm that you can get used to. I found waves coming from off both port and starboard bows and then, rather more alarmingly, random waves approaching the stern. Soon all three sets were getting higher. I found myself energetically spinning the helm to ride the waves ahead and avoid getting pooped by the waves astern. I don't know if my technique was the best. I was working as hard as I could to keep us upright. It was like riding three rollercoasters at once. This carried on for a long time, I have no idea how long, and then just as swiftly the seas became normal again. When things calmed down I asked the skipper, who had stayed below the entire time, why he hadn't come up to the helm.

'It looked like you were doing all right,' he said.

We sailed peacefully into Dartmouth that evening. I'm not normally seasick but after that passage I had vertigo for the next twenty-four hours. I also had a vague recollection of reading about the tidal race around Portland Bill. I later found out we had sailed straight through one of the most dangerous patches of water off the English coast.

I'm not entirely sure why that story sprang to mind, but I suspect it is because writing this book has been rather like being back aboard that yacht. I had no idea what was going to happen when I set off.

The weather was great, the world is beautiful and our destination was clear. All of a sudden we were being battered on all sides. Contemporary events are like that passage, and the inner battle to stay on course is similar.

I have simultaneous urges to explain things clearly, to share my understanding and to write in a way that rewards the attention. But I have to explain that I can't explain. Understanding is not something I can write; it is something each of us must do for ourselves.

To see all of a magic eye picture you must force your eyes to look through the surface.

The surface is pretty too though.

The tendencies of cognitive inertia, abstraction and unemotional objectivity are appealing to policy-makers because they offer a clear picture of what lies beneath our reality. But that is the problem. The clarity is delusional. Abstractions *never* lie beneath reality. They are projected *on top* of reality as a means of analysis. By their nature, abstractions *exclude* data.

There is no necessary limit to the application of an abstraction. If one accepts the validity of an abstract analysis, it is equally valid for a small town or the entire globe. Policy-making facilitates and promotes centralization, and centralization promotes the universal application of policies. Centralization has been the dominant vehicle of progress for approximately one hundred years. Hence our world is overwhelmed by organizations that are Too Big To Succeed.

In 2020 a centrally determined strategy was applied to almost the entire globe. Immanuel Kant, had he lived to the age of 298, would have witnessed a real universal application of his categorical imperative. Would he have been proud? Or would he have recanted?

My early training in hypnosis was fragmentary. Before I found a complete course there were lots of training weekends in large houses in North London. My fellow students were a disparate bunch. There were the lost and the lonely, the serious seekers, the dilettantes, and strangely thin, sparkly-eyed American women of uncertain age.

One day I found myself in a smart apartment in Marylebone with a bunch of enthusiastic NLPers (NLP stands for Neuro-Linguistic Programming). We were excited by the possibilities of our new skills. There was a sense of discovery and adventure in the air.

'If only,' someone said, 'there was some magic substance we could inject into our kids to give them confidence. That would be so great!'

I was nonplussed.

'Well, there is,' I said. 'It's called love.'

There was a stunned silence, then the conversation moved on.

I was very pleased with my clever comment and only realized later that love is half the story. Exactly half. And here is another opportunity for a magnificent diversion which will remain untaken …

Alternatively, I could give you a quick summary of the other half, and how they work together to instil confidence and you would have a neat moment of insight without any depth at all and thus I would cheat you of the opportunity of real understanding by selling you a lightweight imitation.

I'm not going to do that.

Maybe we can talk about it when we meet. Or there's another book to be written here if I can bear it.

Alternatively you can go online. There are a gazillion courses on confidence at once-in-a-lifetime bargain prices. So, problem sorted, no? Everyone is confident now!

Centralization leads to further dissemination of abstraction-based policy. That's been happening for ages, but recent technological advances have made it more pernicious. The circle is made more vicious when the commentariat is possessed by the same tendencies of thought. Policy has supplanted authoritative decision-making, so leaders and systems fail to develop their understanding and flounder from one grandiose blunder to the next. For governments and world organizations, ineptitude is the new normal.

Theorists argue which policy is best. Should we be socialist or free-marketeers? What is the best policy for healthcare, education, housing, energy, environmental protection and so on and so on? They do not consider the possibility that any policy at all will be the wrong approach to a solution.

Much of the time the best option is to leave the authority in the hands of those immediately dealing with a problem and let them arrange an appropriate local solution.

The ability to create and use abstractions is, in itself, neither good nor bad. It is a cognitive tool which is immensely useful in the right context. The problem, put precisely, is not abstraction but the *default prioritization of abstraction.*

In the contemporary ocean of incompetence, malefactors get an easy ride. If all you want is power or money, you will find politicians and academics easy to manipulate. Big Tech, Big Pharma and Big Money prosper mightily.

There is observable in daily life an enormous divide between, on the one hand, ordinary, sensible people doing ordinary sensible things and, on the other, institutional dysfunctionality and deranged public figures.

Consider any contemporary issue which is currently being taken seriously by politicians and ask these questions:

> Does the issue entail belief in one or more simplistic abstractions?
> Does this belief minimize the importance of context?
> Does this belief encourage centralization?
> Are opinions fixed and resistant to change?
> Do the proponents display juvenile and unsubtle emotional states?

If the answer is yes to two or more of the above, the chances are that the issue is misconceived because it is founded on an inadequate abstraction. As we have seen earlier, such issues are exacerbated because:

- Abstractions can induce hypnotic cognitive capture.
- Foundational abstractions may be integrated into the sense of self.
- Foundational abstractions may distort a person's entire world view.

Cognitive capture is not a weird, unusual phenomenon. It is normal. It is, sadly, the everyday state of many people. This is not new. There is plenty of evidence that human behaviour before the impact of literacy was far from perfect. But maybe, just maybe, cognitive capture makes it a bit worse.

The people in those days all understood one another. They came from the East to a plain in the land of Shinar and settled there. They made bricks and they built a city called Babel, or Babylon, and they decided to build a tower that would reach all the way to heaven. They set to work and the tower rose higher and higher. The Lord saw what they were doing and he feared what they might do if they carried on. So he confused their language and scattered them over the face of the earth.

This is usually explained as a myth about the origin of the multitude of human languages.

Maybe it is.

Maybe it is a story about grandiosity, about what happens when you try to reach heaven using earthly tools.

Maybe it is a story about taking techniques that are excellent for a modest purpose and imagining that they are appropriate to master all of creation.

Maybe it is not an explanatory myth but a prophecy, telling us that when we try to go too high with low-level materials it will lead to confusion and chaos.

But, hey, it's just a story.

Except for some people.

For them it is the Word of God.

Science as a career has supplanted science as a vocation. What started in the 17th century as a solitary quest for knowledge has become an industry and a career with all the pressures and compromises that entails. Real science, like real philosophy, has drifted away ...

Science, like all other dominant paradigms of the 20th century – capitalism, technocracy, ideology and democracy – is delivering fewer and fewer of its erstwhile benefits.

Thomas Kuhn believed that science progressed by means of paradigm shifts. It could be said that we are undergoing what Kuhn called a paradigm shift, but it may be more accurate to say we are experiencing paradigm collapse.

Heidegger saw this coming. In an interview with *Der Spiegel* in 1966 he said, 'Only a God can save us.'

Few people paid much attention to this comment, even though it was used in the headline, because in most of the interview Heidegger was trying, and failing, to explain away his antisemitism.

There has been a staggering increase in communications of all sorts, but there has not been a commensurate increase of things worth saying. Enthusiastic sloganeering is a harbinger of the destruction of meaning. Consider these words: Science, Community, Education and Leadership.

The more these words are used, the less they actually occur.

How, *exactly*, does this happen?

It is a consequence of what Heidegger called 'idle talk'.

Idle talk is speech in which we take ideas and phrases from the discourse around us and take them on as our own. Instead of crafting our own opinions we take them, as it were, off the shelf.

Why would we do that? Because we always and everywhere are making meaning, and that can be hard work. It is equally hard work to accept how little we really know.

We have lost the habit of pondering. Interestingly we can become very attached to other people's ideas if we use them to build our world view, but if we are only following the fashionable herd we let them drop easily and leap off again towards the next promising idea.

As idle talk increases, deeper meaning becomes less accessible and the meanings we encounter in the tumult of public discourse become more shallow and fleeting while vigorously proclaiming their depth and importance.

Idle talk is what 'one' says, in German the talk of *das Mann*. Heidegger suggests that much of the time what we say and also what we do is 'what one does'. That is fine if 'what one does' is healthy and functional. What happens if 'what one does' – what social psychologists call social norms – is unhealthy or dysfunctional?

There are four types of people:

> Those who know, and know they know. Listen to them.
> Those who know, and don't know they know. They need to wake up.
> Those who don't know and know they don't know. They need to learn.
> Those who don't know and don't know they don't know. They are a menace. Please stop electing them to public office.

The bread and butter work of qualitative research before the internet was creative development. We would take out cartoons or storyboards of an advertisement to test how people understood them.

The key question was, 'What is the take out?'

The 'take out' is the ultimate impact of the advert.

Someone might say for example, 'Well, it's very clever', but at the same time reject the message of the ad.

The take out is not 'it's clever' but rejection.

Some clients didn't get this. Some discussion groups take place in facilities with a one-way mirror so the clients can observe the group. Some clients would listen intently until a respondent said something that agreed with their own view.

'That's it!' they would say.

As Harry Nilsson's Rock Man put it, 'You see what you want to see and you hear what you want to hear.'

How can we know what is insightful, and what is merely confirmation of our prejudices?

We did some research for a large pharmaceutical company on an over-the-counter remedy for athlete's foot.

We had puzzled long and hard over the characteristics of the different types of buyer of the remedy and created a market segmentation based on their motivations.

We presented the slide of the market segmentation and immediately afterwards the lead client walked out of the presentation. We carried on to the end and then asked his assistant if there was a problem.

Not at all, she replied, the insight in your segmentation chart is brilliant. He got everything he needed from it so he didn't need to stay any longer.

That client was called Joe Heron.

His reaction prompted us to try very hard to create a 'Heron chart' in all our presentations. Joe Heron has gone on to make himself a considerable fortune filling a gap in the liquor market.

The Balinese apparently described the time before Europeans arrived as 'when the world was balanced'. In those days chiefs did not see their duty to promote progress or development but rather to maintain the balance of the world.

We hear more and more about balance these days, and yet it is less and less evident. There is a great deal of discussion about the need to maintain a balance between left and right. However, over the last decade or so, as Colin Wright wittily depicted in his publication Reality's Last Stand, the fulcrum has moved so that what was once on the left is now on the right. There is another problem. Those who wish to redefine balance fail to acknowledge that something more fundamental than a fulcrum is required for balance.

Gravity is required.

Gravity is delivered by reality.

Eventually.

13

A TITLE STORY

Books, unlike stories, really do need titles. As I was writing this book I created a file of candidates. It grew to more than fifteen pages long. More and more titles cropped up but I despaired of ever finding one that felt satisfying.

However, as the book advanced, people began to ask me what it was called. I mentioned one title, *Everything Is Breaking and Everything Will Be Fine*, and a lot of people liked it. After a while it grew more attractive to me too. It acknowledged contemporary collapse while also promising a positive future. If you want to sell a book it helps if people like the title so I began to think I had found it. I adopted it as my working title. One more task accomplished.

As I approached the end of the book I found myself losing momentum and unable to find a way forward. As you can see, up to this point there are plenty of reasons why 'everything' is collapsing, but there is less obvious evidence that 'everything will be fine'.

Reluctantly I admitted to myself that everything will not be fine. Some things will be very un-fine. That is always true in life, and it is particularly the case when an over-ripe civilization is rotting. It would not have been appropriate to say, 'Everything will be fine' in Rome in July 410AD.

I realized I would have to admit to a bit of over-claim for the purposes of marketing.

'Everything will not be completely fine,' I would write, 'there will be some problems, but if you make some good decisions everything – well almost everything – will be fine for *you*.'

That, I thought, is a realistic compromise which will allow me to keep my well-liked title.

I still couldn't write any more though.

I stewed for weeks and weeks trying to work out how to show that 'Everything will be fine' – or even 'Almost everything will be fine'.

In reality, for many of us, in spite of current and future troubles, there will be a great deal that is good, but it is not predestined and I cannot make it happen by writing a magical book.

Eventually I realized, after far too long, that my working title didn't work. It was a lovely, attractive, hopeful, encouraging title for a book. Just not an honest title. As I stepped back from my attachment to the title I noticed other reasons why it was suboptimal. Collapse and renewal are just a small part of what I am writing about. I am optimistic but I can only do my little something. Certainly not the great big everything.

The correct title came to me first thing in the morning after a night of vivid dreams.

As I dragged myself out of the misdirection I had created with my inaccurate title I realized I had fallen prey, yet again, to the traps of language about which I am writing. My working title created two categories: the 'everything' which is breaking and the 'everything' which will be fine. Those categories clarified my thinking. I arranged my ideas to fit inside them. Things started to look neat and orderly and clear. But I could not progress. I was trying to make my book fit the title – fit those categories – instead of having the title fit the book.

I had accidentally hypnotized myself. Again.

I said a sorrowful goodbye to my sweet, well-liked title. It is a weakness of many writers to fall in love with certain ideas or expressions, to be enchanted, to be mesmerized even ... Noel Coward knew it.

'Kill your darlings,' he advised.

I write with the blood of a thousand darlings.

Categorical thinking is deeply embedded in my mind and, I suggest, yours. It is seductive and hypnotic. It is a great challenge to grasp and use categorical thinking without becoming imprisoned within it. Even after I have renounced my simplistic title I find myself struggling over and over again to 'sum things up', to reach a conclusion and tie up the loose ends, and the storytelling part of me fights just as hard to keep talking, to keep revealing and to avoid summing things up.

Maybe I just can't build a castle. Maybe all I can do is go windsurfing. How do you reach a conclusion on a windsurfer? You can reach your destination if you have one, but what if you just went out for a sail? Then, as the saying goes, the journey is the destination. How can you sum that up? How can I sum this up?

Maybe you have been waiting and waiting and waiting and you want to know, *where are we going?! Please explain what is going on.*

The origin of the word 'explain' is the Latin *explano*: to flatten, make level. What if the phrase 'deeper understanding' was more than a mere metaphor? What if deeper understanding really has depth? If so, it would vanish if it were flattened out into an explanation.

That would be sad.

OK, but if we are going somewhere, as children like to ask, *Are we there yet???*

Are we there yet? No. Not quite.

Understanding takes energy, effort and time. Sometimes it requires focus and concentration, at other times we need to relax and let our mind wander elsewhere for a while. It may require some pondering. Often it requires all of the above. Understanding is not just an activity of the intellect. It requires emotional and sometimes physical engagement too. It almost always takes a lot longer to understand something than to read it.

Sometimes we have to hear a story or read a book many times in order to understand it better.

I used to teach Ericksonian hypnosis at various schools of hypnotherapy. I told one of Erickson's stories as an illustration of how different things were in his day. A couple of students came to see him to request his help as a hypnotist. The woman was pregnant and desperate for a termination because she would not be able to continue her studies and she knew her parents would be appalled that she had got pregnant. Her boyfriend fully supported her decision. They wanted to be hypnotized to have the conviction to go through with their decision.

Erickson talked to them for several hours and it was clear that they were firmly determined. Eventually he said that he maybe he would be able to help them if they came back next week. However, in order to receive that help, there was one thing they absolutely must not do. Between now and then they absolutely must not think of a name for the baby.

They came back the next week. They had thought of a name for the baby. The baby was born, the mother graduated a year late, her parents accepted the situation and adored the baby and all ended happily.

I told that story as an example of how Erickson was highly manipulative.

'Don't think of a name for the baby,' is rather like, 'Don't think of elephants.'

To make sense of the command you have to think of the thing you have been forbidden to think about. Erickson's stipulation pushed the couple towards naming the baby and therefore, I felt, having the baby.

I had been telling that story and my interpretation for two years before I realized that I did not fully understand it.

What if after Erickson's words the students had not thought of a name for the baby? In that case they would not have formed an emotional bond to a future child and would have been more able to proceed without any further assistance from Erickson. Erickson did not force a decision, he forced an outcome.

At first glance this abstraction thing seems quite arcane and quite ... abstract. Writing, ancient philosophy, Plato's theory of forms, dusty old stuff really. Curious but scarcely relevant to the brilliant digital wwworld, eh?

On second glance it is outrageous to suggest that something so long ago, something followed by a multitude of other social, political and technological changes, something so simple, something so manifestly good and liberating, could have such problematic and long-lasting consequences. Even if we concede literacy played a part in the development of Greek philosophy, as Havelock argued, we have since had centuries of progress. By now, surely, the collective genius of hundreds of years of brilliant minds will have dealt with any problems or deficiencies.

On third glance, you will discover a threshold effect. Once you recognize the effects of these cognitive biases you begin to see them almost everywhere. Contemporary events in politics, medicine, social movements and corporate and environmental policy all bear the marks of over-valued abstraction, excessively fixed thinking and a lack of both contextuality and emotional understanding.

Many thinkers have been circling around this phenomenon. It is not so outrageous to see that Havelock and Heidegger are discussing the same event, albeit from very different points of view.

Julian Jaynes and more recently Iain McGilchrist have proposed neurological explanations for cognitive phenomena which can perhaps be more parsimoniously explained by the impact of writing.

All the gods were living in a palace at the top of a huge mountain. At that time Vishnu was the boss. He had to go away on business so he called all the gods together and said, 'I'm going away. Behave! And don't open the door until I come back.'

Then he strode off down the mountain.

The gods all started running around and playing and having a high old time and after a while there was a knock at the door.

The nearest god ran to the door and opened it.

There on the doorstep was a small green creature with fangs and claws and horns and an evil look in its eye.

'Ugh,' said the god, just a little bit scared, and he took a step back.

As he stepped back the creature grew a little bigger.

'Ah!' said the god, stepping back again.

The creature grew bigger again and took a step forward.

'Help, help!' said the god and he ran back into the palace. 'Help! There's a monster!'

The creature, which did indeed look like a monster, walked into the palace and the gods all peered at it from the balconies and passageways and right there in front of their eyes it grew bigger and bigger and bigger.

The gods all began panicking and the monster grew even bigger, filling up the palace and lashing its tail and gnashing its teeth.

Pretty soon the gods were all squashed up against the walls and the monster was getting so big he was cracking the roof.

At this moment Vishnu returned.

'Good grief,' he snorted. 'What are you doing?'

'What?' said the gods. 'We … I ... it, it's ...'

As they mumbled the monster shrank a tiny, tiny little bit.

'Don't you know what this is?' blasted Vishnu.

'We ... uh … no …'

'It's a fear monster! It lives on your fear!'

The gods blushed and blethered and the monster shrank and shrank.

Pretty soon the gods were feeling much better and the monster had shrunk right down to the size of a mouse. The god who originally let it in, picked it up by the tail and sidled towards the door.

'Hey!' Vishnu beckoned him. 'I don't think so. I think we will keep him around. Then we will all be able to see if you get too fearful.'

From an academic point of view, this book is a frivolity. It has no references to the latest papers in the premier journals and makes countless assertions without supporting arguments. It does not state its goals nor advance a clearly defined thesis. It refers to thinkers from different disciplines with minimal introduction and without situating them in the history of the fields in which they worked. It discusses philosophy but behaves like a parkour delinquent scrabbling over the roofs of ancient debates without deigning to descend inside and engage in serious discussion. It includes anecdotes and stories without explanation or analysis.

More charitably one could say this book is a wasted opportunity. If its many claims were to be addressed with rigorous academic discipline, an interesting and valuable contribution could be made to genuine academic research.

From another point of view, academia is in a sad state of decay, drowning in its own protocols without the courage to step back from the dross and irrelevance created by its over-expansion and by the erasure of critical debate by careerist expediency.

Many good minds have been caught up in misguided tolerance of under-achievement. Many are reduced to policing the trivia of protocol and steer clear of judgement. All this and more was already problematic long before the arrival of woke politics. There is still much good work but the rise of banality is remorseless.

More charitably we could say that academia is rather like politics: people go into it with the best of intentions but the system undermines them.

It would be absurd to blame all humanity's ills on literacy. The Buddha lived and taught in an oral society. His teachings indicate there is an challenge inherent in being human. The problems of wrong action, wrong thinking, attachment, the monkey mind and so on all predate writing.

The Buddha's teachings were considered so insightful and so useful they were memorized by his disciples and written down about three hundred years after his death.

Clearly being human has always been a challenge, but perhaps in modernity we have exacerbated it. What if many modern problems arise not so much from the incoherence of our self but from our notion of the self itself? Have we invented a self without sufficient internal structure to hold it together? Could it be that unless we create ties and buttresses to hold it together, the self is just a space through which our passions parade?

If so, then here lies the great appeal of ideologies and abstraction. Abstractions, and better still ideologies, offer us an artificial but largely coherent self.

The more you look, the more you see.

Heidegger claimed that the most basic way in which we meet things in the world is that we use them.

Both Luria and Everett agree that the organizing principle of oral peoples is utility. For oral peoples the purpose of life is simple – survival and then enjoyment. Maslow's pyramid is reduced to two layers: the essentials of existence, then above that have fun.

Luria in his fieldwork discovered that his pre-literate respondents did not have a modern sense of self.

When he asked one man, 'What are you like?', the man replied, 'I don't know – you have to ask someone who knows me.'

One of his researchers asked a young woman what she thought of herself.

'I am a bad person,' she replied.

'Why is that?' he asked.

'Because I only have one dress,' she replied.

The researcher tried again. He asked her to think about herself, not her possessions. Could she talk about herself? What, for example, would make her a better person?

'Two dresses,' the woman replied.

The dialogue above is my memory of what I read and right now I cannot get to the library to check the exact words. I am telling you the story how I remember it.

Each one of us has lots of evidence of the incoherent self. Everyone who has woken up swearing not to touch alcohol for a week, for a month, for a year or ever again and found themselves having a drink the very same evening knows what it is to be incoherent. Everyone who has made and then broken a resolution knows about incoherence. Everyone who has looked up a reference online and found themselves browsing elsewhere half an hour later know about incoherence.

So let's look at the issue from another angle. Given the evidence of our incoherence, why did we ever believe that we are coherent?

Clearly at several levels we are coherent. Social roles corral our waywardness. Jobs dictate a great deal of our behaviour. Traditional etiquette controls some of us some of the time.

Many of these controlling factors are losing their sway but we mostly forget our own incoherence and imagine that we are somehow a unitary being. The monkey mind is evidence of our incoherence, but like a teenager screaming, 'I *am* an adult!', we are childishly attached to our delusions and don't want to admit what we really are.

Unexpectedly, my years of wondering and wandering led me to some sort of an answer to the question that occurred to me in Arizona all those years ago. It is not a definition – that would be weird given all

I have said about abstractions – but I reached a viewpoint on the nature of human being.

It may have already occurred to you that the idea of 'the self' is itself an abstraction. We have observable bodies and characteristics and names and so on but the self is a way of talking about ourselves that is extremely useful (see?) but cannot be isolated and examined in the real world any more than a soul can. It is an idea.

So what are we?

What are we? On the one hand a ridiculous question: I know who I am and you know who you are and that is perfectly adequate for us to live our lives. We have a formal, legal identity which pertains to our bodies and is catalogued in passports and identity cards.

On the other hand it is a great mystery: what is the fundamental nature of our being? Why did the ancients counsel 'Know thyself'?

There are three popular analogies for human being. Ivan Pavlov's famous experiments conditioned dogs to salivate when they heard a bell ring. His work led to the theory of behaviourism which sees us as creatures that can be conditioned to respond to stimuli. We are like dogs. There is a lot of truth in this, but it is not the whole truth.

We are like onions, it is said, because there are many layers to our psyche. Beneath the many masks we wear in society and the sediment of years of conditioning lies our true self right at the centre of the onion. There is something valuable in the idea of many layers, but there is more aspiration for than evidence of an inner, true self.

More recently we have been likened to computers, machines that run programs and analyse data. I use this analogy when I write about the bug in our programming language.

These analogies – dog, computer, onion – all have their merits, but all are limited, and if pushed too far misleading. We are obviously bodies and yet more than bodies. A body is a necessary but not sufficient condition for our being. We are *a process*. We are whatever it is that stops when we die, and yet leaves behind a body.

Heidegger's magnum opus was titled *Being and Time*. Let's talk about the 'Time' bit.

Warning: Philosophers will note the section below is very far indeed from a complete and rigorously accurate summary of Heidegger's ontology of *Dasein*. Non-philosophers are warned that it introduces a notion of being so peculiar and unorthodox that you may struggle to get your head around it. If it gets too bizarre, just skip to the last line.

As we saw earlier, Heidegger starts his analysis of *Dasein* (his word for human being) with the observation that our primary meeting with things in the world is that we use them. We understand what a thing is because we know what it is for. I know what a hammer is even when it is just lying on the work bench. I can use a hammer for hammering a nail. Every 'what I can do' is a possibility.

Understanding is founded in possibilities. A possibility is what is not yet, but may be in the future. Every possibility is a possible *future*. We are understanding, and understanding is *essentially futural*. Thus Heidegger proposes that our being is constituted by the future.

You will remember that Heidegger also claims that we always have some mood or other. Your mood, or feeling, tells you how things are going with you or, in the telling idiom, 'where you are coming from'. Your mood is the upshot of what has happened. For Heidegger, in our mood we manifest our past.

And of course we are present in a world within which things and other people are accessible.

So, Heidegger proposes, we are temporal phenomena: 'always already ahead of ourselves as having-been, alongside the being of others.'

So far, so weird. In *Being and Time* it gets a whole lot weirder. The deeper exploration of our temporality is fascinating if you are that kind of a geek but we now have enough for our purposes here: **our being is a kind of temporality which stretches into the future whilst carrying over the past and being open to entities in the world around us.**

Let me ask a question. What else has this shape? What is structured by its future, has some feelings of how things are and opens a world of context around us?

I'm going to answer my own question.

A story does that. Until it comes to an end, a story always makes sense as heading to the future, always solicits feeling and always offers us its world. A story is a profound analogy for human being. We are much, much more like stories than we are like dogs, onions or computers.

The similarity between our own being and the being of stories makes stories instantly recognisable. We can overhear just a couple of words, 'and *then* …', and we can feel the flavour of the story and the expectation to hear what happens next.

Furthermore, this is why we can understand so much, by means which are completely different from explanation, when we are transposed into a story. We can experience a story in the same mode that we experience our being in the world.

In therapy there is a benefit in knowing that we are very like stories. We are not things that are damaged by traumas in the way that a machine is broken by a sledge hammer. We are an ongoing process. Bad things can happen in a story, yet the story itself can be wonderful.

By the same token, the pursuit of a 'real' self is ultimately the pursuit of a delusion. We can all learn and develop integrity and become better in all sorts of ways without trying to become a particular version of an abstraction.

We are not like characters in a story. We are like the story itself.

I met Peter Brook again in 1985 when I cycled to Avignon to see the opening performances of his masterpiece with Jean-Claude Carrière, a staging of the *Mahabharata*. The original epic in Hindu is fifteen times longer than the Bible. Brook and Carrière reduced it to a mere nine hours – three plays of three hours each. The plays were performed on consecutive evenings, but also, once a week, one after another taking the entire night.

When I saw *The Conference of the Birds* Brook had invited me to see it again on the following night. I declined the invitation because my host in Paris had organized a dinner party for me that night. I didn't enjoy the dinner party knowing I could have been watching that marvellous show instead. I didn't want to make the same mistake with the *Mahabharata*. I had tickets to see the whole show three times.

It has been said that all of Western literature is a footnote to the *Mahabharata*. Every story you can think of is included within it. The overarching story is of a long conflict and eventually a great battle between cousins, the Pandavas whose king is Yudhishthira, and the Kauravas led by Duryodhana.

Brook kindly gave me an interview which I sold to help pay for my trip. I was particularly struck by one remark. He told me that in the thinking behind the *Mahabharata* the very same words could have a different meaning depending on the quality of the person who speaks them.

The show was performed inside a quarry several kilometres outside Avignon. Raked seats looked down on to the playing area. At the back was the quarry wall, and at the foot of the wall was a waterway. There was a small pool down stage. The ground was beaten earth and sand. When characters came on with flaming torches all four elements were on stage: earth, air, water and fire.

I sat waiting for the all-night performance to begin. The scheduled start time had passed. People were bickering over seats and all around me people were complaining. The atmosphere was dreadful. I was agitated by the agitation around me.

Peter Brook walked into the centre of the stage. He stood completely still. The audience fell silent. Brook explained that there would be three intervals. After the first play there would be half an hour – long enough to get a snack and a drink. After the second play, twenty minutes, long enough to stretch our legs and for the thirsty to get a quick drink. Then there would be one more break, just long enough to make a quick run to the loo.

By the time he had finished talking the audience had been transformed. There was a gentle appreciative expectation. Brook walked off stage and a few moments later the show began.

After nine extraordinary hours, I realized why the show had started late, at exactly the right time. The cast walked quietly into the space beyond all battles, beyond suffering, beyond all killing and being killed, and knelt at the water's edge to set little candles afloat.

Brothers and cousins, victors and vanquished, embraced one another. The musicians played an exquisite melody as we witnessed that final paradisical scene and the light of dawn bloomed over the edge of the quarry.

14

A PLAUSIBLE CONCLUSION

There is no Big Answer.

From time to time it looks as though there is a Big Answer, but it is an illusion, a virtual image generated by many little answers working at the same time.

Not only is there no Big Answer, but Big is the biggest problem.

You can see now that every attempt at a Big Answer goes wrong for the same reasons that policies and protocols all eventually fail. Central control promises efficiency, best practice and cost savings and undermines authority, trust, context and competence.

A centrally controlled protocol may prevent many small mistakes. But when such a protocol is itself mistaken its impact is far greater than a single local error. It is also more difficult to correct than a single wrong decision, because it must be investigated and assessed before change can be approved, and it is probable that vested interests will fight against change.

Finally, Big Answers almost always destroy the little, local answers that used to work pretty well.

Philosophically this book is phenomenological. That means that you can observe what I am asserting for yourself in your own life. In theory, that should mean that all phenomenological expositions are indisputable. If I see X and you see X, we have to agree that there is X.

Unfortunately, as Heidegger noted, perception is not that simple. It must always already involve some interpretation. We can only see X as X if we have some notion of X in the first place and we may have differing notions. If the means by which you interpret the world already includes abstractions, your entire world view could be distorted. If you are unaware of the abstractions, and of their consequences, you will consider other points of view to be plainly wrong or mad.

Of course, this may also be true of me.

Corr Willbourn Research did several pieces of work for the various bodies that control the water industry in the UK. It was an interesting challenge. It is difficult to get people's opinions about something they don't think about. We devised a form of deliberative research wherein respondents did their own research, had time to think about it, then came back to share their thoughts in a dynamic workshop. You can still find some of that work on the internet if you search hard enough.

At some point, in some far distant part of public sector procurement, something had gone wrong and it was decided procedures had to be tightened up. We were asked to go through a process to be on a roster of 'approved' companies. We logged on to an online questionnaire which had pages and pages of questions about our finances, our pay scales, our different grades of pay scales, our capital reserves, our company procedures and so on and on and on and on and on.

Fewer than 15% of the questions concerned our research competence. I lost patience with the process and we never completed that questionnaire. I later learned from one of our clients that she had strongly counselled against the questionnaire. She was ignored.

That episode in itself is not worth writing about, but pseudo-meaningful nonsense such as this keeps armies of bureaucrats employed, undermines the authority of commissioners, rewards pointlessness and pedantry and drives out competence and creativity. Millions of trivial incidents such as this underlie the decay of the West.

A plausible conclusion from this book up to this point is that a minority among us, beneficiaries of a balanced education, achieve some degree of autonomy in some, if not all, areas of their lives. For the rest, the default state of mankind in modernity is incoherence, held together by weakening social norms, ideologies and hypnotic abstractions.

It's not a flattering conclusion and there are plenty of opportunities to deny, distort or diminish it, which is exactly what most of us do most of the time.

That's a bit bleak.

Is there anything more positive to be said?

Yes, there is.

All around us there are millions of people living well. The real solutions to our problems are small and local and proportionate. Furthermore, it is millions of people doing small, local things well that generate what appear to be Big Answers to Big Problems. The apparent 'Big Answer' is an emergent phenomenon, like a murmuration of starlings. The birds all flock together and create beautiful shapes but they have no leader, they are just following a few simple rules.

I have written elsewhere how simple rules of greed, fear and unconsciousness can create great evil. (See the notes at the back for a reference if it interests you.) Are there any simple rules that create great goodness?

This is a constant question in philosophy, in psychotherapy and in everyday life. What should I do? What are the rules?

You won't be surprised to hear that I am wary of proposing rules for success. I wouldn't need to write all this if I could just write out the rules. But for those who like a little more straightforward guidance, here are just a few starters dug out from between the lines. Think of them as suggestions or perhaps notions to bear in mind …

ONE

Don't mistake abstraction for understanding.

TWO

Beware of hypnotic abstractions.

Those are both negative. In terms of positive guidance I offer four more suggestions below. I did not invent them. We are all climbing the same mountain, so in different ways and in different words they have been proposed by greater men and women than me for centuries. They are perhaps no more than common sense. Yet strangely it seems we need frequent reminders of common sense.

THREE

Discernment. Each of us needs to cultivate discernment, to see things more and more clearly. An enquiring intellect is not enough. We need to develop our emotional understanding, stay curious and try to understand a little more.

When I am teaching I use the mnemonic 'Head, Heart and Hips'. Simply put, we have three modes of understanding – intellectual, emotional and physical – and they are fostered by an education that includes literacy, storytelling, apprenticeship and experience. We understand more clearly when we use all three modes.

The process is cumulative and unending. As Sharon put it many pages above:

'You start as a beginner. You get to be intermediate. Then, at last, you are advanced. Then you realize you are a beginner.'

FOUR

Proportion. In a way this is a subset of discernment, but it is so important that I give it separate billing. We can make an effort all the time to keep our perceptions and our responses proportionate to each other and the context of the world about us. We may focus our attention on a single entity but we must try also to see how and where it fits into the bigger picture. Sometimes we have to adjust our point of view, sometimes we have to adjust our response. Great suffering is caused by our lack of proportion. It is foolish, as Mr Gurdjieff put it, 'to burn down the house to roast a pig.'

FIVE

Principles. As noted earlier, principles solve a lot of problems. Basic, functional principles are very simple indeed. For example: be fair and be polite. Try also to be kind and honest. It can be hard work being kind. Being honest is also difficult given our capacity for self-deception, but both attempts repay the effort.

Perhaps I need to clarify here the difference between a principle and a policy. They are both, strictly speaking, abstractions, and perhaps they overlap, but a distinction I find helpful is this:

- Policies, ideologies and protocols dictate specific behaviour. They require you to do as you are told.
- Principles offer some guidance on what to do or how to do it, but they do not dictate your actions. A principle requires you to assess your context and make your own decision.

Principles are always important. It is far too easy to be carried away by grandiose campaigns and believe that, for example, fairness and politeness are dispensable. A lot of the problems about which people start grandiose campaigns evaporate if enough people are fair and polite.

SIX

Make up your own mind. Don't follow my advice or anyone else's without checking it makes sense for yourself. And check again later. Things change. You will make plenty of mistakes, but over time you will make far fewer than if you simply do what is normal.

If a group of people follow these suggestions they will be independent, diverse and de-centralized. They will be a wise crowd.

These suggestions may be helpful but they are far from exhaustive. Maybe there will be far more important suggestions that are not written here.

There is, for example, much more that could be said about trust and boundaries, and negotiation, rhetoric, influence, projection and responsibility and so on, but the more specific the advice, the more carefully we have to note exceptions and limitations and fend off more and more possibilities of misunderstanding. Perhaps we can explore those ideas in another forum.

There is also much more that could be said about these turbulent times. I have my own opinions, strong ones at that, but they don't belong here. This is a ragged, rugged path towards a possibility of personal understanding. The possibility, and the understanding, are yours to do with as you wish.

Oh ... that sounds a bit pompous, doesn't it? Or patronizing, perhaps?

I completed my PhD twenty-five years ago. Only in the last few years have I begun to understand with my heart and my hips what I discovered with my head. It is frustrating to discover how little I can share. However much food there is in the larder, we can only eat one meal at a time.

Jesus, who we are told had infinite power and a far greater message than mine, spoke about the same problem: 'I speak to them in parables: because seeing they see not; and hearing they hear not, neither do they understand.'

On the other hand, I am not important. All around you is all you need to understand more deeply. The truth is hidden everywhere. Everything catches the light and has its shadow. Even in modern universities, for all their faults, there are still some rigorous, original thinkers, and great teachers tell stories, create experiences and use elements of apprenticeship. Good scientists still work and get published in spite of the circular, self-corrupting nature of peer-review.

So how can we know we are getting it right?

We can't.

We really, really can't.

Religious people solve this conundrum by replacing the question with belief in God. If you believe in your God, you follow his rules and that is what is right. You have faith. Still not knowledge, but faith.

Actually, even for the religious the question keeps cropping up – but it is transformed into a problem of faith. Do I really, really believe in my God when terrible things happen that make me question my faith?

For the irreligious the question remains: 'How can I know I am doing the right thing?'

And the answer remains: 'You can't.'

So you decide.

Place your bet, take responsibility and get on with life, while keeping enough humility to admit you may be wrong. You win some, you lose some. But the more you take responsibility, the better you get at winning.

Every day we may struggle to achieve consciousness, to fight our way out of the hypnosis, out of falling into the automatic ways of the world, out of falling into delicious, palate-pleasing unconsciousness.

Sometimes we have to hear, or read, things many times to understand them better.

I have been reminded over and over again as I write this, how much cannot be written. To learn to dance, we must dance, to learn to love, we must love, to learn to live, we must live.

Eventually there are battles we must fight, however reluctantly. Before then, before the Great Battle, here, from Vyasa, the character whom Carrière made his narrator for the *Mahabharata,* is the advice he gave to the Pandavas as they set off into ten years of exile:

> Go. The forest land is vast. Profit from exile to see and listen. Walk. Pause beside wise men. Question savages and madmen. Listen to stories; it's always pleasant and sometimes it improves you.

All around us are many balanced people who contribute to the common good. You can know them not by their qualifications or politics or proclamations but by paying close attention to the effect they have on those around them. The right action at the right time tends to avert drama rather than cause it, so it is not always easy to notice a wise person, like, perhaps, an old man with a walking stick. Nonetheless, keep looking. They are worth seeking out. They are the lights to guide us through dark times.

This book comes to an end. However, if you wish, it could be the beginning of something else. If there is a demand for it, I will be travelling and consulting and talking and meeting people and telling stories and running workshops.

If you would like to talk or listen or meet or ask questions, please join my mailing list. The sign-up details are at the very end of the book. Please let me know where you are. That will help me know where to go and help us to create a community. We might even make ourselves a wise crowd.

Legend has it that the inventor of chess presented the game to the emperor of India (or China). The Indian (or Chinese) emperor was delighted.

'What can I give you as a reward for this magnificent invention?' he asked.

'Your Imperial Majesty,' replied the inventor, 'I would be grateful if you were to give me some rice. Please give me just one grain for the first square on the board and two for the second and then double again for each square thereafter.'

'Is that all?' asked the emperor incredulously. 'That's a bit unconventional. Don't you want your weight in gold? Or my daughter's hand in marriage?'

'No, your Majesty,' replied the inventor, bowing deeply. 'That is all I want.'

'Very well,' said the emperor, and he turned to the Head of the Imperial Household. 'Give him what he wants.'

Servants started to measure out the rice and very soon there was not enough rice in the Imperial Palace. The Head of the Imperial Household called for more from to be brought from the provinces. Gradually it dawned on him that there would not be enough rice in the entire Empire of India (or China). In fact, there would not be enough rice in all of India and China. By square 64, there would not be enough rice, even today, in the whole world.

Mathematicians tell this story to illustrate the power of exponential growth.

I am inspired by this brilliant inventor. In these days the internet has come to dominate marketing. Influence and riches flow to the celebrities with the most followers. Being young, hot and female is marketable like never before. Having a ripped body or a slick, hip, online product or catchy social commentary is highly monetizable.

I'm not young, nor hot, nor female. Nor am I ripped or slick or hip or capable of an ongoing stream of witty, topical commentary. I do not expect to trend online.

Instead I am asking you, dear reader, to do me an old-fashioned favour.

I hope someone gave this book to you. Perhaps you bought it yourself. Perhaps you are even the very first person to have bought it. If you have had an insight or two, if you have been inspired or amused, if you have had a laugh, or an 'aha' moment, ask yourself,

'Would my world be a better place if other people felt what I have felt? If other people saw what I have seen? If other people had a laugh or two, or a moment of thinking differently? Or even if other people read the same book and achieve very different understandings?'

If you value what you've received, pay it forward. Buy two more copies and give them to two people: one whom you think will really enjoy it, and one whom you think could really benefit from it.

Wait!

Don't do it straight away. A realistic assessment of the value of this book will arrive when you find yourself thinking about it, seeing things differently or telling one of these stories in a week's time. If something sticks, if you pick it up to read again, if anything from this book still sings to you in a fortnight, a month or a year, then you will know it was worth reading. When it occurs to you that if more people understood even a small part of this it would make a tangible improvement to our lives, that's a good time to buy a copy for a friend – or even an opponent.

So if you would like more people to see things differently, give away two copies of this book. This will be way more effective than liking a post on the internet or giving me a good review online – but please do that as well if you wish.

Don't do it if you are too short of money. But if you do, and every other reader does so too, and we assume that on average you take two weeks to buy the books and everyone takes one week to read it, then in a year's time there will be over five hundred thousand copies out there. That will be enough to ensure that I can set up seminars and talks so we can explore storytelling and understanding and hypnosis and being and negotiation and all sorts of intriguing and useful things further together somewhere near you.

In eighteen months' time there will be 134 million copies in circulation. That represents one copy for everyone in Mexico or one copy for everyone in the United Kingdom and in Thailand, and I will be able to travel all over the world to run workshops. Three weeks later there will be enough copies for all of Mexico *and* the United Kingdom *and* Thailand.

That will be great, but it gets greater. In ninety-six weeks' time – that is less than two years – there will be a copy for every person on the planet. Also by then a few hundred million people will have been given multiple copies, so it will be OK if a few people with no spare money drop out. It will still work.

Incidentally, as maths geeks will already have noticed, at ninety-six weeks doubling every three weeks we will have reached the equivalent of only square 32 on a chess board, i.e. half of the board. The emperor had another 32 squares to go. But you can stop. When you and everyone you know and everyone you meet already has a copy of this book it will have become more popular than the Bible and Chairman Mao's Little Red Book. Time to move on. Or for me to write another book.

You may think this blatant self-marketing is outrageous and completely out of place in a respectable book. On the other hand, almost every significant voice on the internet urges you to click and subscribe with every post. I am doing the equivalent, with the same mixture of self-promotion, and smiley, lightweight, self-interested nudging. But of course I believe, as I'm sure do all those online influencers, that there is a real benefit in my product.

The hugeness of the world that leans on us through the internet often makes me feel that whatever I do could never be enough. I am too small, my understanding is too intermittent and the unconscious energies of fear and greed are too powerful. But we can make a difference.

When I talk with friends I feel better and when I work with people sometimes we can do something good.

What would happen if millions of people read this book and half, or a third, or a quarter or even 10 per cent of them were to feel a bit better, think a little differently, have a few more moments of understanding, or became a little more willing to trust themselves to learn and a little less willing to be dazed by abstractions and experts? What if some of those people got together?

What might happen then? Is this a path to the great awakening?

Wait!

What was the ending of that story about the chessboard inventor?

Did the people of India (or China) starve so that the emperor could pay his debt?

No.

The emperor made the problem go away. He had the inventor executed.

My wife saw a draft of the early chapters of this book and read the story of Markandeya, a story she has heard me tell many times. She was put out.

'I know you wrote it,' she said, 'you chose the words ... but here it is so ... so flat.'

Perhaps if you read that story again you could do me, and yourself, a favour and read it out loud. That is how people used to read, by the way. Silent reading is a very modern habit.

Next time, maybe see it as pictures in your mind as you read it.

Then don't read it.

Tell it – just to yourself the first time. See the story in your head and, in your own words, say what you see. Don't try to be fancy. Just feel what you feel and tell it as clearly as you can.

Then go and tell it to someone else. See the story in your head and simply tell what you see and remember,

'No titles! No morals!'

NOTES AND SOURCES

I have avoided hardcore philosophizing in the book, but there is plenty of it lurking in the forest. If you are interested in exploring further, get thee to Google Scholar. The notes below include details of books and journals quoted in this book. If you are specifically interested in my work you could take yourself to City University, London, in the UK, and read my PhD thesis. You may have to queue. The library only has one copy.

Alternatively you can contact me via hughwillbourn.com to explore the possibility of publication, talks or seminars to explore the philosophical forest in more depth.

Chapter 1

Page 5 Uncommon Therapy is an excellent introduction
Haley, J., *Uncommon Therapy*, W. W. Norton & Company New York 1977

Page 11 I worked mostly in the old British Library Reading Room
Heidegger, Martin, *Being and Time* (*Sein und Zeit*), tr. Macquarrie and Robinson, Basil Blackwell, Oxford 1962. Martin Heidegger was one of the two most innovative and influential philosophers of the 20th century. He was also at best politically naive, at worst a

repugnant antisemite. His influence on philosophy has been so vast that it cannot be expunged, but a good number of critics believe his contribution is undermined by his political failings. The other great philosopher of the 20th century was Ludwig Wittgenstein. The two belonged to vastly different schools of philosophy but Wittgenstein was probably closer in his thinking to Heidegger than is commonly understood. Consider this: 'The aspects of things that are most important for us are hidden because of their simplicity and familiarity.' Wittgenstein, L., *Philosophical Investigations,* Blackwell, Oxford 1953

Chapter 2

Page 15 In 1996 Carl Sagan was interviewed on television
https://www.youtube.com/watch?v=jod7v-m573k&t=38s

Page 19 I spent months wandering in the Narnian wardrobe of orality
Lord, Albert, *The Singer of Tales,* Harvard University Press, Cambridge MA 1960. See also: http://nrs.harvard.edu/urn-3:hul.ebook:CHS_LordA.The_Singer_of_Tales.2000

Ong, Walter J., *Orality and Literacy: The Technologizing of the Word,* Methuen, London 1982

Page 19 Havelock proposed that Plato's philosophy
Havelock, Eric, *Preface to Plato,* Blackwell, Oxford 1963

Page 20 In the *Phaedrus,* Plato tells us a curious story
Plato, *Phaedrus and the Seventh and Eighth Letters,* tr. W. Hamilton, Penguin, London 1973

Page 23 The basic form of language is sound
Lord, Albert, *The Singer of Tales*, ibid

Chapter 3

Page 38 Again, I hope it is popular but I am not popularizing academic psychology
My favourite introduction to applied psychology is Robert Cialdini's *Influence: Science and Practice*, Allyn and Bacon, Boston 1984

Page 41 The internet presents another fascinating diversion
https://www.hughwillbourn.com/post/cc4-lss2-we-can-do-better-than-follow-the-science and https://www.hughwillbourn.com/post/9-a-little-knowledge-is-a-dangerous-thing

As for others' viewpoints, there is too much to summarize here, but a good place to start is Nicholas Carr's *What The Internet Is Doing To Our Brains*, Norton, New York 2010

Page 41 The internet augments the pressures and distortions
Mander, Jerry, *Four Arguments For The Elimination of Television*, Quill, New York 1978

Putnam, Robert, *Bowling Alone*, Simon and Schuster, New York 2000

Page 42 This society upholds a fierce technological idealism
Mander, Jerry, *In the Absence of the Sacred, Sierra Club Books, San Francisco 1992*

Chapter 4

Page 46 A hundred years ago more people were still unaffected by literacy
Jung, C.G., *Analytical Psychology*, Random House, New York 1968

Page 47 'We think here,' he said, indicating his heart
Jung, C.G., *Memories, Dreams, Reflections*, Pantheon, New York 1963

Page 47 Walter Ong's research was focused on the nature of orality
Ong, Walter J., *Orality and Literacy*, ibid

Page 47 Ong's work pointed me towards Alexander Luria
Luria, A.R., *Cognitive Development: Its Cultural and Social Foundations*, tr. Martin Lopez-Morillas and Lynn Solotaroff, ed. M. Cole, Harvard University Press 1976

Page 49 In 2007 Daniel Everett published *Don't Sleep, There Are Snakes*
Everett, D., *Don't Sleep, There Are Snakes*, Profile Books, London 2008. For an introduction to Everett's academic work, see 'Cultural Constraints on Grammar and Cognition in Pirahã', https://www.journals.uchicago.edu/doi/abs/10.1086/431525

Mainstream linguistics when Everett was a student was dominated by Noam Chomsky's notion that the basic structure and limits of language are hard-wired into us all, and each language is just a variation on this 'universal grammar'. Everett found that standard Chomskyian linguistics did not seem to apply to the Pirahã language. His findings seemed to support Edmund Sapir's earlier thesis, at that time out of fashion, that the structure of a language affects its speakers' cognition. Linguistics geeks will note that my proposal about literacy is a fairly strong variation of the Sapir-Whorf hypothesis.

Page 51 You may remember that Martin Heidegger claimed
The significance of utility opens a vast field of potential historico-philosophical enquiry that stretches to the horizon and beyond. Entire careers could be played out in just the first few kilometres. It is one of many such fields for which there is no room in this book.

Page 55 He took the Humberside Police to the High Court
The full story is here (https://www.mailplus.co.uk/edition/comment/137338/the-enormous-free-speech-victory-of-an-ex-policeman-intimidated-over-his-trans-tweets) and it is worth reading.

Page 55 Following my High Court victory
You can hear Harry tell the whole story here: https://twitter.com/SpeechUnion/status/1472880095220142081

Page 57 Let's go back to around 900 BC. King Solomon
1 Kings 3:16–28

Page 61 In *The Wisdom of Crowds* James Surowiecki collected evidence
Surowieki, J., *The Wisdom of Crowds*, Doubleday, New York 2004

Chapter 5

Page 69 You can read the bones of that story in another book
Abjørnsen, P.C. and Jorgen Moe, *The Complete and Original Folktales of Abjørnsen and Moe*, tr. Tiina Nunnally, University of Minnesota Press, 2019

Page 69 Back in 2003 I wrote
McKenna, Paul and Willbourn, Hugh, *How to Mend Your Broken Heart*, Bantam Press, London 2003. Reissued as *I Can Mend Your Broken Heart*, Bantam Press, London, 2006

Page 71 In his deeply unconventional study of being, Heidegger
Heidegger, M., *The Fundamental Concepts of Metaphysics, World, Finitude, Solitude*, tr. William McNeill and Nicholas Walker, Indiana University Press, Bloomington 1995

Page 72 Listening to a well-told story
'Meaning and Narrative: a Phenomenological Enquiry, with reference to Psychotherapy', Hugh R. Willbourn. Submitted for the degree of Doctor of Philosophy, City University, London 1997

Chapter 6

Page 76 On a weekend in April 2011 I found myself on the Tweed Run
https://www.classicdriver.com/en/article/tweed-run-2011-quiet-revolution

Page 76 Lindy Hop is a dance form created by Black Americans
Manning, Frankie and Millman, Cynthia, *Frankie Manning: Ambassador of Lindy Hop*, Temple University Press, Philadelphia, 2008

Page 76 By the 1950s Lindy Hop had fallen out of fashion
https://swingstep.com/courses/history-of-lindy-hop/lessons/myth-busting-the-revival/

Page 79 There were, and in a few special places there still are
Quotation from Mander, Jerry, *In the Absence of the Sacred*, ibid

Page 79 As Professor Dreyfus of the University of California, Berkeley put it
Dreyfus, Hubert, 'Anonymity versus commitment: The Dangers of Education on the Internet', *Educational Philosophy and Theory*, vol.34, no.4, Nov 2002

Page 80 The training of both nurses and doctors includes
https://dailysceptic.org/2022/08/02/the-real-reason-the-nhs-is-failing-hint-nothing-to-do-with-covid-or-lack-of-funds/

Page 80 Nurses used to gain a diploma after years of work and instruction
https://www.nurses.co.uk/blog/reasons-nurses-leave-retention-survey/

Page 81 This is not merely my opinion as an outsider
O'Mahony, Seamus, *Can Medicine Be Cured?*, Head of Zeus, London 2019

Marsh, Henry, *Do No Harm*, Weidenfeld & Nicolson, London 2014

Page 81 These critiques are not unusual
https://dailysceptic.org/archive/what-is-the-nursing-and-midwifery-council-doing-about-nursing-shortages/

Page 86 I had found a real unconscious bias
https://www.nationalreview.com/2017/01/implicit-bias-debunked-study-disputes-effects-unconscious-prejudice/, https://nymag.com/intelligencer/2017/12/iat-behavior-problem.html

Page 89 The single most effective treatment for alcoholism
https://www.healthline.com/health-news/alcoholics-anonymous-is-still-the-most-effective-way-to-deal-with-alcohol-addiction

Chapter 8

Page 103 This hypnosis does not require a hypnotist
Wittgenstein, L., *Philosophical Investigations*, ibid

Chapter 10

Page 120 As mythologist Joseph Campbell put it
Campbell, J., *Pathways to Bliss*, New World Library, Novato, California 2004

Page 120 I was a teenager hanging out
Bennett, J.G., *Witness: The Story of a Search*, Hodder and Stoughton, London 1962

Page 125 In a TV interview in 1952, aristocrat and philosopher Bertrand Russell said
https://www.youtube.com/watch?v=xL_sMXfzzyA

Page 128 Gurdjieff described the mission
Gurdjieff, G.I., *Beelzebub's Tales to his Grandson: An Objectively Impartial Criticism of the Life of Man*, Penguin Compass, New York, 1999

Chapter 11

Page 140 Jung saw this coming
Jung's commentary in the introduction to *The Tibetan Book of the Great Liberation,* first pub. 1954, Oxford University Press 2000

Page 141 Ernest Hilgard, another prolific researcher of hypnosis
Hilgard, E.R., *Divided Consciousness: Multiple Controls In Human Thought and Action,* John Wiley and Sons, New York 1977

Chapter 12

Page 146 The world's most famous woozle is an academic paper
https://www.conservativewoman.co.uk/exposed-the-97-of-scientists-agree-with-manmade-global-warming-lie/

Paper by John Cook *et al* at: https://iopscience.iop.org/article/10.1088/1748-9326/8/2/024024

Page 149 One day I found myself in a smart apartment in Marylebone
Neuro-Linguistic Programming is a mode of psychological intervention devised by Richard Bandler and John Grinder from the work of Virginia Satir, Fritz Perls, Milton Erickson and others.

Page 151 The people in those days all understood one another
Genesis 11: 1-9

Page 155 We hear more and more about balance these days
Colin Wright's website: https://www.realityslaststand.com/p/shop

Chapter 14

Page 175 I have written elsewhere
https://www.hughwillbourn.com/post/23-cock-up-conspiracy-or-murmuration

Page 178 Jesus, who we are told had infinite power
Matthew 13:13

CONTACT

To buy more copies of this book, to find out about seminars and workshops, to be on the mailing list or to join our wise crowd go to:

www.hughwillbourn.com

In due course you will be able to purchase other books and even, perhaps, merchandise.

All details about products, services and special offers will be posted and updated there. Please do get in touch.